ANOTHER DAY IN PARADISE

Living on Tybee Time

Ben Goggins

Photojournalist, Activist,
Marine Biologist, Philanthropist

Published by:

Maudlin Pond Press, LLC
PO Box 53, Tybee Island, Georgia 31328, USA

ISBN: 979-8-9857239-0-8
eBook ISBN: 979-8-9857239-1-5

Introduction

Forty years ago we moved to Tybee. And we never looked back. This little island is a slice of paradise, and in this book you will come to see why.

For a decade now I have written a column in the Savannah Morning News called "Looking for Pearls." In this book are some of the pearls about Tybee.

Get ready to reset to Tybee Time. Get ready to relax and fall in love with this place, with the people who live here, with the sun and wind on the sea oats, with Tybee's mystery and romance.

I am honored that so many Tybee folks have these articles pinned to their walls and tucked in their scrapbooks. These stories are timeless windows to a blessed way of life.

Get ready to marvel at pirates, pelicans, turtles, and coyotes. Cemeteries, shells, and sailors. Singers, tune-up artists, painters, and poets. Get ready for things you expect to find and for things you may find hard to believe about another day in paradise.

I hope that you find here the stuff that dreams are made of.

Ben Goggins
January 2022

Why we love <u>**Another Day in Paradise**</u>:

Ben Goggins' stories and observations of Tybee's authentic and quirky flavor and the unique characters who call it home always bring me a smile or a sense of awe. He captures the spirit and essence of Tybee. You feel as though you know, or want to know, the people he writes about, and that you are part of this magical journey that many locals call "Tybee-time" - where time stands still or doesn't really matter!

> Shirley Sessions,
> Mayor of Tybee Island

Ben sees the space between the lines, the silence between the notes. Ben's world includes the magical spots that many of us overlook in our hustle-bustle pace to get through the day. Ben shares his vision with a unique talent all his own.

> Monty Parks,
> Tybee Island City Councilman

I love this book. Even when you leave Paradise, a little of the sun, the sand, the sea clings to you. A breath of sea air, a seagull gliding on a breeze - such things are here for you to enjoy. Ben's writing illuminates the stories, and the stories will lighten your heart until you can come back. Read and listen as the tide comes in.

> The Rev. June Johnson,
> Vicar, All Saints Episcopal Church

This book makes my day.

> Brent Levy,
> City Arborist and unofficial sunrise
> photographer

Table of Contents

1

Red Lights at Night

On dark summer nights faint red lights often hover in the dunes just above the reach of high tides. They come from loggerhead sea turtle project volunteers watching nests which are soon to hatch.

1

Red Lights at Night

It's a record-breaking year for red light districts on Tybee. No, not those kind. These the police will actually help you find. They're free, family-friendly, and staffed by teachers and retirees.

In the dark, where the dunes meet the beach, the flickering red lights that you can barely see are signs of dedicated Turtle Project volunteers. Like midwives and nurses, they are there to watch over hatching loggerhead turtles.

Over the years I have seen the nests along the beach, carefully marked and fenced. But not until the night of July 17 did I ever witness the miracle of turtle birth. A neighbor told me a nest on the North End was hatching and to look for the red lights. It was a moonless night, and the volunteers' flashlights looked like dim red vigil lights in a chapel.

Four volunteers were there, quietly waiting around the nest. They had already carried five turtles down to the water and had named them as they went, after "I Love Lucy" characters. An hour later, another little turtle emerged from the coarse sand, flapping his little flippers and seeing the world for the first time. "Little Ricky." I left about 11:00 PM, but the volunteers were staying the night.

The next night was what turtle-watchers live for. It's what they call "a boil." From the churning sand forty-five turtles came out in a matter of minutes. The volunteers placed them in buckets. Once the boil ended, they carried them down to about ten yards from the water's edge. One volunteer got in the water and turned on a soft white light to attract them. The sight of those turtles moving like a throng of happy children toward the waves, black shapes against the wet sand, is unforgettable.

Like babies in the womb hearing their mother's heartbeat, they've heard the rhythmic pulse of the waves for 60 days. And now they scramble toward the ocean.

Tybee's project leader is Tammy Smith, a teacher at Marshpoint, who's been doing it for eleven years. She has 96 volunteers this year. From May through August, they make dawn walks over Tybee's 5.4 miles of beach to watch for new crawls. They check each nest daily and pay special attention to signs of settling near the end of the incubation. Then they stay the nights once hatching begins. Nights that are hot, muggy, and buggy. It's real dedication to an endangered species. They do it because it's a calling. I'm not surprised that so many are teachers. And they drive from Isle of Hope, Pooler, Savannah, and Springfield.

Another night, another nest, the day after a boil, Kevin Sofa and Julie Kirk watched and waited. One straggler came out and clambered about ten yards in the wrong direction, toward the lighthouse. They took him down to the water, and he still was going in that wrong direction. Kevin got in the water and turned on his white flashlight. The very next step that turtle hung a right and made toward the sea.

August 3, at a nest near 8th Street, Cheryl Tilton and Amy Capello, answered onlookers' questions while several turtles emerged. Laura Walker from Savannah was there with her son Palmer; she said that "seeing this completes a cycle." Three years ago on the night of her fortieth birthday, walking on the beach at Jekyll Island, they saw a mother turtle laying her eggs. Palmer was three then. Loggerheads begin reproducing at about age 35. When Palmer is his Mom's age, he may see one of these hatchlings come back to Tybee.

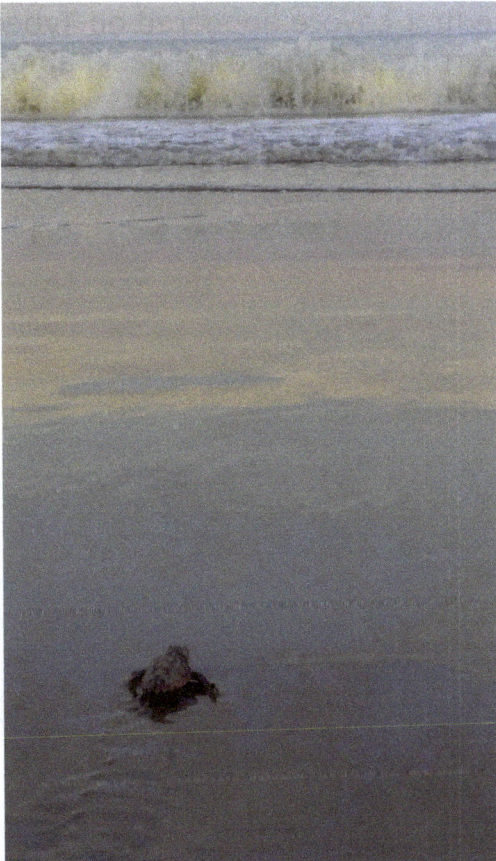

2

Coyotes Come to Town

When the first coyote appeared on Tybee Island, having trotted from Fort Pulaski across the Lazaretto Creek bridge, residents were nervous. What might become of the island's cats?

2

Coyotes Come to Town

Three weeks ago late on a Sunday afternoon I came face to face with the Tybee coyote. And he looked a lot sharper than I did.

I had been doing yard work and was dirty, worn out, and looked like I had been running through the woods. The coyote looked like he had just showered and was on his way to Southwestern night at the North Beach Grill.

Since the coyote was reported a while back, I had been hoping to get a glimpse of him. I was keeping an eye out for him around twilight. Cruising slowly around the out-of-the-way, woodsy, marsh-side neighborhoods where he had been seen.

So it was a complete surprise to see him trotting along in broad daylight, comfortable in the center of the road in front of Officers Row. He looked confident and relaxed, like he had just won Best in the Wild Dog Class at the kennel club.

I lost him while I ran to get my camera.

A family vacationing from Cleveland said there are lots of coyotes in the National Park near them. They said that this one looked much cleaner than the ones they usually see. And that he held his tail up higher. Marks of his east-of-Lazaretto lifestyle.

Coyotes appeared at Ft. Pulaski about five years ago. And it's a habitat they like. Gloria Lee, Chief of Interpretation, said that they have gradually and naturally spread eastward across the country. The Park Service practices a no-interference policy, leaving the animals and the food chain alone.

She said there have been no negative interactions with employees or volunteers. And no confrontations with any of the many dogs that people walk there every day.

Betsy Plageman from Tybee was walking Frosty, her 116-pound white German Shepherd. She said that she had seen a coyote pass through a group of deer, who didn't flinch or stop grazing.

Ft. Pulaski carpenter Jerry Turner said he often sees coyotes crossing the roads as he makes his morning rounds. And a year ago he heard about seven of them howling from different directions as a helicopter passed overhead.

Both coyote parents take care of and feed their young. Jerry thinks that there is at least one breeding pair on Pulaski, with three pups seen this summer.

He hasn't noticed any overall impact on Pulaski's deer, except that there seem to be fewer fawns. Coyotes mostly eat small mammals, like rabbits, raccoons, and mice.

But they love fruits and nuts too. Wild plums, blackberries, persimmons, black cherries, and pokeberries. And farmers know that they will tear up a watermelon patch, eating a watermelon down to the rind.

I walked the trails and dikes of Ft. Pulaski last week, hoping to photograph the coyotes. I saw plenty of beautiful deer, but no coyotes. I did see tracks of coyotes, deer, and raccoons. And coyote droppings, full of rabbit or raccoon fur.

Ms. Lee pointed out that coyotes have a natural fear of humans. SSU softball Coach Jim Dodd, a volunteer at Ft. Pulaski, said that he came upon four coyotes one night. They appeared to be stalking a single deer. He shouted, waved his arms, and everybody took off.

I didn't get a coyote photo, but Ms. Lee gave me a good one from Ft. Pulaski. And Forest Service biologist John Kilgo sent me several from near Augusta.

Coyotes are essentially nocturnal. Native Americans have long cherished them as clever creatures, respected for their intelligence and survival skills.

The gates to Ft. Pulaski close at 5:15 PM. I'm not giving up. But my guess is that the coyotes come out at 5:20.

3

A Pirate Raid

October is pirate season on Tybee. During the rowdy Pirate Fest, one plank the pirates walk is into the island's nursing homes.

3

A Pirate Raid

Berkeley Grady is an angel. The second one I've known who's been the Activities Director at Oceanside and Savannah Beach Nursing Homes on Tybee.

The first was our neighbor years ago, Betty Obert. Betty loved the residents under her care. And I know that miracles happened there every day because of her kind heart.

Betty liked to say that friends of the Nursing Homes were her "lovely neighbors." Now Berkeley manages to attract volunteers and neighbors to enrich the lives of residents.

And who is my neighbor? Therein lies a parable of the Good Pirate.

For five years in a row a group of pirates from St. Augustine has visited the Nursing Homes when they come up for Tybee's Pirate Fest. I saw the high-spirited, high-energy group in action last month.

Those guys take over a room. Dressed for the run-way, not the plank, their hair and make-up were perfect. They were the theme. They danced and mingled with residents at a great afternoon party. They brought with them their adventures on the high seas, their colorful life of running blockades and daring escapes.

They spent time with each resident, sharing their stories and listening too. The music, food, and atmosphere kept everyone smiling, laughing, and dancing. Afterward the pirates went from room to room, visiting bedridden residents who had not been able to come to the party.

Berkeley says that residents look forward each year to the Friday party and the Saturday parade that passes in front of the Nursing Homes. "The entire Nursing staff, especially the CNA's, is the team that makes the party possible. They get the residents ready; they see to every detail. They are the true angels and treat every resident like family."

Paul Devivo, founder of Pirate Fest, says the St. Augustine pirates are a good-hearted group, always ready to do whatever festival organizers ask. Firing their cannons at events. Raising the pirate flag at City Hall and kidnapping the mayor. Carrying the King and Queen on their ship, the Black Heart.

They used to visit St. Michael's School before it closed, fascinating the students and talking about pirate history. Answering questions about their dress, swords and pistols, ships and sails. They will be naturals to visit the Tybee Island Maritime Academy when it opens next Fall.

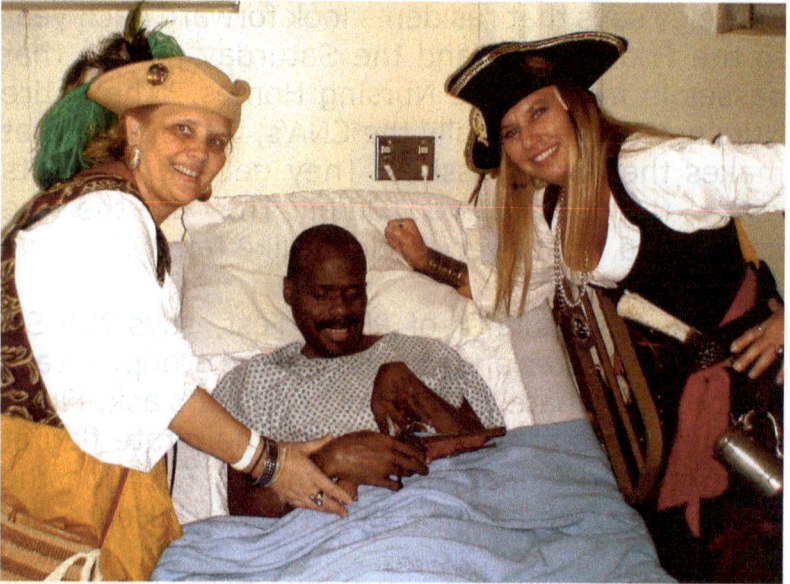

Phil Reed, the leader of the St. Augustine crew, says that they are serious about being authentic and educating the public. They have participated in re-enactments around the country and even in England, commemorating the Revolutionary War. And aboard the HMS Bounty, which sank during Hurricane Sandy.

Berkeley says that the pirates are a blessing, a breath of salt air, for the residents. And that, week in-week out, the involvement of volunteers and people of good will makes all the difference.

Campers from the Burton 4-H Center came often this Summer. Socializing, serving coffee and snacks, bringing along turtles, leading a conga line.

Marty McKenzie and His Love Ministries come regularly to sing hymns and entertain with puppets and clowns. Popular visitors Esther Williams and Robin Evans come every week to give free manicures to men and women.

Four people come in with pets. A beagle named Raisin. Coco, the hound dog. Other visitors come by to play the piano every week.

An Old Savannah Tours trolley takes residents for a tour of downtown Christmas lights each year. And for rides in local parades.

Stacye Jarrell and Oceanfront Cottage Rentals gave the pirates free lodging this year. And the pirates looked after Berkeley's Beloved Community.

Pirate Phil said, "We are good pirates. We always try to leave more treasure than we take." Last month in Tybee's Nursing Homes, I'd say, "Mission accomplished."

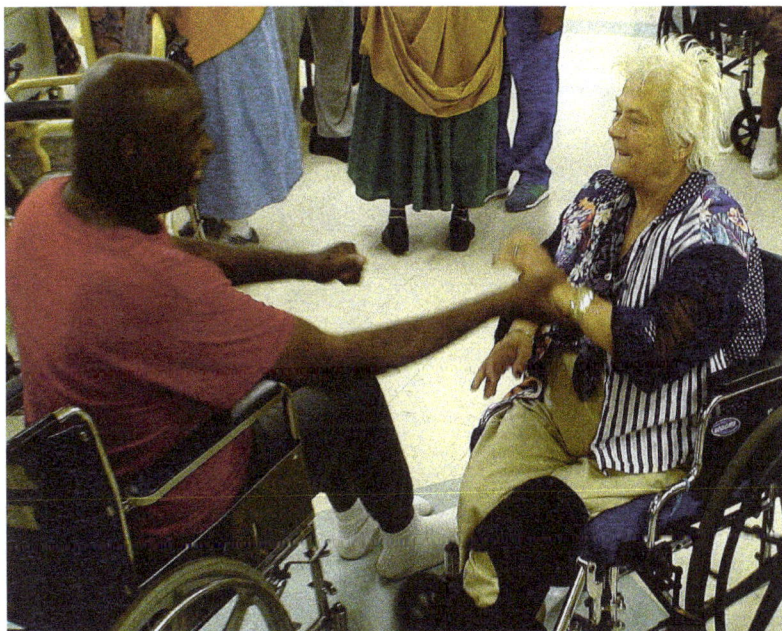

4

Between Two Bridges

The drive on Highway 80 from Bull River to Lazaretto Creek is a journey to another state of mind. Buzzards and boats make for musical notes.

4

Between Two Bridges

Sometimes when you come over the Bull River Bridge on the way to Tybee, you see something there before you that takes your breath away. Noah's Ark in an Iowa corn field.

Actually it's one of the huge container ships that come every day up the Savannah River. It's an illusion, but from the bridge, your line of sight makes it look like it's on dry land. In the late afternoon the marsh grass glows like amber waves of grain. And there, just over the trees, a ship seems to sit.

That four-mile stretch of the Tybee Road from the Bull River to the Lazaretto Creek is always a pleasant drive. With expected views and nice surprises.

Just past the Bull River Bridge, along the roadbed to the old steel bridge, there's an area where a group of vultures hangs around. Doing what, I probably don't want to know. Networking, I'm sure.

A few months ago, I glanced their way and was stunned to see two bald eagles, perched on the 'No Dumping' signs, just watching the vultures. Talk about getting your attention. I pulled over and took a few low-tech cellphone photos before they flew off in the direction of Wilmington Island.

And the birds go on. "Like a bird on a wire." The birds on the power lines write an ever-changing tune and a soundtrack to Tybee.

Years ago my wife's good friend Sister Angela Collins told her about watching the sun go down over the Forest River behind the Carmelite Monastery. She said that she loved to see the long, graceful strings of pelicans gliding home over the marsh.

She said they were like rosary beads and carried her thoughts where they needed to go. They were her evening prayer.

After that, we saw the birds on the Tybee Road differently too. Spread out on the power lines, their silhouettes look like musical notes on a scale.

Fat doves for whole notes. Starlings, mockingbirds, and sparrows as half notes, quarter notes, eighth notes. Sometimes a big cormorant next to the pole as a treble clef.

I don't read music, but I think they must make a song of some sort. Maybe it's just the "Jaws" theme. But I like to think that it's something more pleasing like "my huckleberry friend." Something the hawks can hear as they look down from the tops of the poles. Or the kingfishers who perch alone on the bottom lines, scanning for minnows.

Lately there have been big swarms of blackbirds that whoosh back and forth over the road, between the cedars and the palms. Escapees from an aviary perhaps. They have bands on their ankles, but they've filed the numbers off.

They put me in mind of the London girls who filmed a once-in-a-lifetime murmuration of 100,000 starlings as they canoed on the Shannon River last year. Those girls, whose website is "Islands and Rivers," were truly in awe, worshipful and silent in the thrill of what they saw.

Sometimes it just takes somebody telling you something, like Sister Angela's way of looking at birds. To give you a new ritual, a new insight, a new beginning.

At the end of "The Prince of Tides," Nick Nolte's character talks about crossing the bridge toward home. At the top of the bridge, he always says the words "Lowenstein, Lowenstein," the name of Barbra Streisand's character. Because she saved him.

Coming over the Lazaretto Bridge, there is the Cockspur Lighthouse to the left. And the shrimp boats at the docks below. The Agnes Marie and the Christina Leigh.

It's then that I like to say my wife's name.

5

Beauty and the Beach

Nobody comes to Tybee because they have heard how great the litter is. Volunteer litter warriors keep the beach clean. One university beauty queen inspired a motivated group of her fellow students.

5

Beauty and the Beach

On the Saturday morning before Easter I went down to Tybee's North Beach to see what jellyfish had been left behind by the night's high tide. What? Doesn't everybody?

There were quite a few adorable jellyfish, but not a bit of litter. The beach was squeaky clean after a contingent of students from Savannah State had gone over it.

They were led by Miss SSU, Tiffany Hallback, a senior Business Management major. And this Queen and her Court were getting their hands dirty, doing one of their "Tigers Keep Tybee Tidy" Beach Sweeps.

Tiffany said that they partnered the clean-up with the Tybee Beautification Association. "We get lots of participation from the Student Government Association, the Marine Biology Club, the SSU Eco-Tigers, Student Orientation leaders, all sorts of groups and individuals.

"This clean-up we have guys from Alpha Phi Alpha fraternity. In February, we had a huge beach sweep at the South End, with about 50 students from Kappa Alpha Psi fraternity and Delta Sigma Theta sorority.

"That sweep was like a dream sequence. It was a very foggy morning, and everybody looked like ghosts on the beach. But we felt warm and fuzzy, leaving the beach looking so good.

"There were about 30 volunteers from Gulfstream there too. We worked in teams that time and recorded what we picked up. I think each volunteer collected over 10 pounds of trash. Lots of plastic ware, energy drink cans, bubble wrap, Styrofoam, snack bags, all sorts of stuff that people should have put in the proper receptacles."

The students I saw were all serious and thorough. And each had their own litter specialties and collecting techniques.

Eagle-eyed Gabrielle Ivory stood on the dune crosswalk and scanned the nooks and crannies for cigarette butts. She was spotting them from 50 yards. "I try to educate people about cigarette filters; they aren't biodegradable like paper is. They're actually a plastic, cellulose acetate, and can take decades to decompose. Birds and fish accidentally eat them; they've even found filters in the bellies of whales."

Professional tutor Corliss Best was picking up around the old diving bell in the North Beach Parking Lot. He said he loves the fresh air and hates to see a beautiful view ruined with trash.

Danial Grant, another senior Business Management major, was working solo around the scenic beach swings. With one continuous motion, expertly plucking up beer cans and plastic soda bottles with his Trash-Gator grabber and popping them into his trash bag, he looked as smooth as Usain Bolt after the finish line.

Towering Sophomore Class President James Ofori said he was interested in anything that helped the community. And that he takes pride in "doing random acts of green-ness."

Tybee resident Jim Glass was picking up near the Shrine Club. He's been participating in beach sweeps for 12 years and said that enthusiastic college students are always a big help.

Tiffany said that they never know what kind of lit-ter they will find. I told her that a few days earlier I had seen my first-of-the-season Pampers, in front of Fannie's in the Strand parking lot, simmering on the sidewalk.

She didn't miss a beat. And said that, since they still had time, they were going down to the Pavilion to clean up and have that area looking good for the next morning's Easter Sunrise Service.

And she said they'll be back on Sunday the 14th for another Beautification Sweep, rain or shine. Waves of orange and blue moving across the sand. Leaving only their Tiger footprints.

I am impressed by their ongoing commitment in all kinds of weather. It's good to know that neither rain nor hail nor fog shall keep these "litter carriers" from their appointed rounds.

6

Elvis Saves the Day

A boy from Honduras loves turtles and saves 15 diamondback terrapin eggs for incubation. Tybee police always brake for turtles.

6

Elvis Saves the Day

I met an ecstatic little boy from Honduras last week who had just found out that he saved 15 turtles. How he did it was simple and something anyone can do.

His name is Elvis Centeno, and he was at the Tybee Marine Science Center. The previous afternoon, his family had been stopped in traffic near Chimney Creek when Elvis spotted a Diamondback Terrapin on the road shoulder. From its size, he knew it was a female.

She had just been run over and was still alive, even though her shell was badly broken. Elvis got out, picked her up, and they whisked her, on Elvis' lap, back to the Center. They left her there with aquarium curator Mike Partridge.

He had not been able to save her. But he had been able to save her 15 eggs; they were intact and not crushed. He had taken them to Armstrong's Biology Department where they will be incubated. And, after they hatch in about 60 days, they will be released back into the marsh.

Elvis' father, also named Elvis (after you know who), said his son loves turtles. Part of why they came to Tybee was that little Elvis hoped to see a Loggerhead Sea Turtle nest or crawl.

He had been excited to see the young Loggerhead swimming in one of the Center's aquariums. And he was really surprised to see so many Diamondback Terrapins of varying ages. They have adults, a two-year-old, and some newborns.

The two frisky 2013 hatchlings were found on the beach by lifeguards. They probably accidentally floated out on a raft of marsh grass on the last Spring tide. For their first few years, young terrapins live in the high marsh, under the dead marsh wrack along the tidal creeks. Dining on crabs, worms, snails, and plants.

The adult terrapins hibernate in the marsh mud during the winter. And swim in the creeks the rest of the year. They have strong site fidelity, staying in home waters year after year. From May through July the females lay their eggs, and that can put them in harm's way.

That is why there are "Turtle Crossing" signs from Bull River to Lazaretto Creek along the Tybee Road. To alert motorists to slow down and watch for the females who commonly cross the road as they look for just the right sandy high ground to nest.

John Crawford with the Marine Extension Service on Skidaway Island says that Diamondback Terrapins are among the most intelligent of turtles. And that they have incredible variety in the designs on their shells.

He assists a group of dedicated Landings volunteers who transfer eggs laid in some of the golf course sand traps to safe hatcheries. Last year they rescued 1000 eggs and had 900 healthy hatchlings.

Diamondback Terrapins are protected in the state of Georgia. Tybee Police Captain William Moseley showed me the "I Brake for Turtles" bumper sticker on his minivan.

"We urge motorists to drive safely and watch for terrapins crossing the highway. Our officers will stop traffic when they see one." He told me how last year, after an incorrect report as to a terrapin's location, they had four cars out looking for the vulnerable turtle.

At the Marine Science Center educator Cody Shelley took time from a squid dissection with a Savannah school group for me to take a few photos. Their two adults are named Pearl and Ruby, and she said they had very mild dispositions.

The Center's two-year-old and the newborns haven't been named. Elvis said he is thinking of fifteen different names. Diamondback Terrapins can live for about thirty years, and he hopes that all of the eggs he saved will enjoy a long swim.

7

What's in a Bougainvillea

Bougainvillea bushes thrive on Tybee. They might make you a millionaire. Their red bracts can look like spiders or tongues of fire depending on the limits of your imagination.

7

What's in a Bougainvillea

OK, for $1 million, who was the first woman to sail around the world?

You asked the audience, and they leaned toward Maria Magellan. But the 50-50 eliminated her and Diana Nyad. Now who is your phone-a-friend?

I'd go with one of the students at the Tybee Island Maritime Academy. They are into that sort of thing. And, hint, Tybee is covered with bougain-villeas.

Her name was Jeanne Baré. She sailed in 1766 with the first French voyage to circumnavigate the globe, led by the Count de Bougainville. And she did it with a little trickery.

Regulations did not allow women on board ships in those days. But her boyfriend was the expedition botanist, and he sneaked her aboard as his assistant, disguised as a man.

In Rio de Janeiro, she became the first European to observe, collect, and describe the tropical plant that we know as the bougainvillea. She named it for Admiral de Bougainville.

Tybee is something of a fertile crescent for the beautiful plant. In the ground, they will grow from hanging-basket size to the size of Volkswagens in a year.

I walked along recently with Tybee Maritime Academy board member Kay Fortner and two students as they surveyed some of the bougainvilleas that bedeck the North End.

She said, "This kind of living lesson ties together marine science, history, and the ecology of the coast."

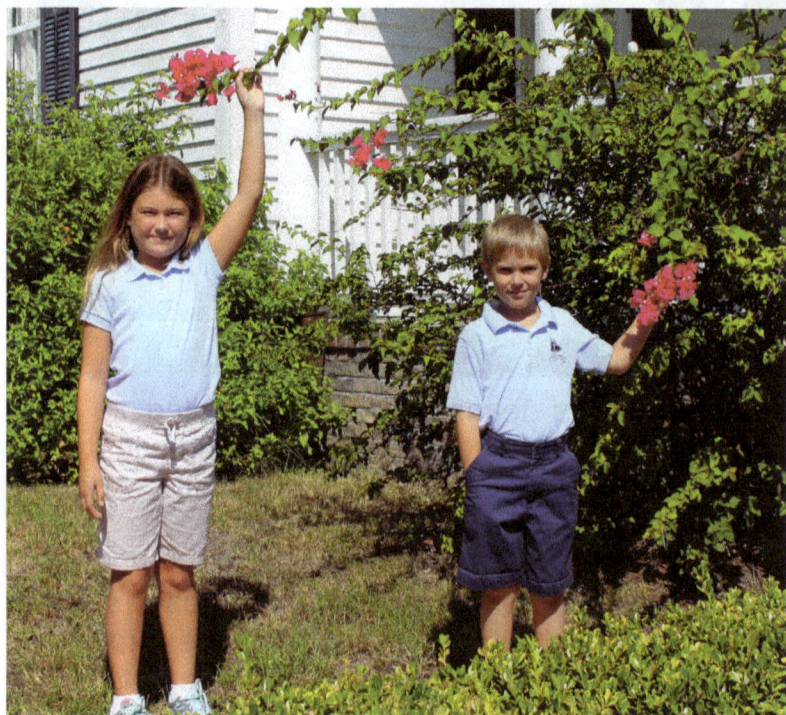

The students were enjoying the sunshine and the science. Third-grader Caroline Efird said she loved the magenta bracts, which looked like her aunt's lipstick. And first-grader Caleb Rimes thought they looked like red spiders in the morning. (Remember, he's in first grade.)

Our dear friend Sister Angela Collins used to have a bougainvillea hanging outside her room at the Carmelite Monastery. She said people who had visited the Holy Land told her how abundant they were there. And legend has them being woven to make the Crown of Thorns or being Moses' burning bush.

But she said that, to her, they were like the Pentecost plant sung about in an old spiritual. And that, suspended above you, their red petal-like leaves seemed to dance like tongues of flame, wanting to brush the top of your head.

Retired Extension Service agent Ed Poenicke says there used to be splendid ones in the greenhouses at the Bamboo Farm, but that their long, arching, thorny branches got to be a problem, snagging visitors.

He jokes that they are perfect to have next to your house to discourage peeping Toms. President Nixon loved them around his home in San Clemente because he said they were a good hazard to the paparazzi.

Chica Arndt, who manages the Savannah-Ogeechee Canal Museum, says that in Venezuela they are called "trinitaria," for the three small cream-colored flowers inside the crimson bracts. Villagers in the mountains call them "little volcanoes" because they look like they are spewing hot cinders.

Tybee is the hot spot, but bougainvilleas do well in Savannah in sheltered locations like downtown courtyards and hugging warm South-facing walls. Chrissy Earl says that tourists often take photos of the bougainvillea that frames her doorway in Savannah. Eric Roden has been told that some motorists drive up Habersham just to see the sprawling bougainvillea that clings to the side of his home on 53rd Street - especially when his blood orange tree next to it is full of fruit.

At Tybee, 5-year-old Ryder Small loves the looming 15-feet-tall purple bougainvillea at his grandmother's home on Shipwatch Lane. He has seen rabbits resting under it.

And I think that, if Uncle Remus had set his tales on Tybee, there might have been a variation where Brer Rabbit was asking Brer Coyote not to throw him into the bougainvillea patch.

8

Mystery Birds - Mystery Road

Locals call Highway 80 the "Tybee Road."
On any given day it is punctuated by eagles or
vultures or feral cats, along with hoboes or
mannequins or Greek priests.

Mystery Birds - Mystery Road

"The Tybee Road is like a recurring dream you are happy to have again and again. It's a familiar place where you drift along on your memories, with the stories of your parents and grandparents like the wind beneath your wings."

That's how Fr. John Caparisos put it when I bumped into him and his wife Sophia on the McQueen's Island Trail on a foggy afternoon last month. It's a peaceful stretch any time, but he said that the fog made it feel more spiritual. Like a friendly ghost.

They had just witnessed an eagle swoop over the channel and grab a trout. They asked if I had seen the Berry College Eagle Nest Cam up in North Georgia. When they were dating as undergraduates, they often walked the nature trails at Berry.

Oh yeah, I've been watching the Eagle Cam (www. berry.edu/eaglecam) every day since the two eggs were laid in January. Me and millions of other surrogate aunts and uncles around the world, viewers from Holland to Israel to Iran to Australia, according to the company handling the live streaming.

It's amazing how you get into pulling for the devoted parents, as they constantly adjusted the eggs, and how you take one last look every night before your own bedtime to confirm that all is still well. The big news one night was seeing the mother fend off a lightning-fast attack by a great horned owl. (On that issue, Fr. Caparisos had divided loyalties since, as a teenager, he raised an orphaned great horned owl for over ten years at his home.)

You'd see the mother sleeping on her side and rocking back and forth. Maybe just getting comfortable, but maybe having a dream herself. And the father vigilant at midnight with the wind blowing his feathers, his eyes glowing in the infrared light of the camera.

The first egg hatched on February 22. The Eagle Cam Facebook page declared, "We have a bobblehead." Lots of people saw it live because, on the night before, the father had fed the female on the nest, which indicated that hatching was near, and he stood watch on a nearby branch.

It is great family viewing. On the eve of the hatching, a Facebook post showed 7-year-old Ariana Galindez holding little eaglet ornaments she had woven, and two flat weaves as nests with white splotches in them as eggs.

I would have named the hatchling Ariana, but Berry named it B3. Last year's two eaglets were B1 and B2 (Berry One and Two). It's coincidental, but I was almost named B3, after one of my mother's prenatal vitamins; it's catchy, but I am happy that ultimately, I was named after my grandfather.

At one day old, B3 was surprisingly attentive and looking strong. During some polar nights, the mother slept with her head turned and tucked between her shoulder feathers, like you see ducks do. And you'd cringe and shiver as the cold winds swept over the nesting adults.

You notice things as B3 grows. Like how he prefers resting his head on his right side. And how, at three weeks old, his feet look way too big, like a clown's. And when he puts his wings by his side, since they are not covered with feathers, it looks like he is putting his hands on his hips.

Fr. Caparisos said that Berry is setting up three more wildlife cams, in a bluebird box, in a beehive, and over their deer herd. He said he'd love to see a cam over the Tybee Road that you could tune in around the clock.

He mused that the drive to Tybee is in his Savannah DNA. He has written songs about the ribbon of highway over the marsh, about the old railroad, and about the French Bakery that used to be next to Chu's.

It is easy to connect to nature and history on the way to Tybee. A big osprey nest sits high atop the light pole where Islands Expressway meets Highway 80, above the appropriately named Robert McCorkle Flyover. And the pair there now are looking pretty parental.

The cell tower next to Davis Produce is usually full of vultures, networking like they are on an old-time

party line. And there is a surreal look to the old Williams Seafood site. All that remains of it are the two tall sago palms that flanked the restaurant's entrance. Guarded now by a strange blonde mannequin in a lifeguard chair. Man, they had a great fresh tomato salad.

Like they have for ages, pelicans and cormorants bask in the sun on the pilings of the old Bull River steel bridge. And just beyond lies a desolate stretch of blacktop that was the old two-laned Highway 80.

On its shoulders are tangles of Carolina jasmine and blackberry vines, piles of stones that resemble old prospector claims, and remnants of hobo fires, complete with rusted tin cans. Majestic hawks perch on the telephone poles and watch the marsh below.

And the pageant of birds over the marsh ebbs and flows. Throngs of starlings swoop and tumble. Noisy grackles thrash around, making a racket in the palms. And moments later sit quietly on the power lines, their bills pointed straight up like innocent choir boys; butter wouldn't melt in their mouths.

You see ibises gliding in for a landing, their long beaks dipping downward like a squadron of French Concordes. And white egrets shining on the mud flats.

Some sunsets are so majestic that cars pull off the road to take pictures. And, if you're lucky, you may see the full moon rise over the road ahead.

And how can you not have wanderlust as ships sail down the river to the sea. With names like the CMA E'toile, the Baltic Panther, the Frisia Rotterdam. Or the Vecchio Bridge, the Paris Express, and the Helvetia.

Just before the Lazaretto bridge, on another spur of the old road, you might glimpse what looks like a windfall of tangerines under the palm trees. But up close, you see that they are orange plastic containers, single-serving Meow Mix wet cat food.

There is a small colony of feral cats there that Tybee cat lovers feed twice a day. The population is dwindling as a result of the spaying and neutering program. The cat folks even give them the occasional catnip toy. And those cats have a savvy look as they walk along the roadside, sort of like they are looking for coins.

Maybe to raise funds for a Feral Cat Cam.

9

Tybee Loves Loggerheads

Endangered loggerhead sea turtles are living treasures found on Tybee beaches. Life-sized fiberglass loggerheads are found in special places around town, courtesy of local artists.

Tybee Loves Loggerheads

When you are coming home after a while away, there is always a special landmark as you approach, that stands out as the signal that Home Sweet Home is close. For my wife and me, it's forever been the Tybee Lighthouse. Like ships she guided to safety in bygone days, she still lights the way for many a Tybee heart.

Gliding down the island side of the Lazaretto Creek Bridge, on your right is the Welcome sign, graced by the big loggerhead turtle Caretta caretta, painted by artist Renee Heidt. Any tourist worth their salt stops to pose with her.

Then, in the twilight, getting closer to home, at the end of Campbell Avenue, on the porch of the historic Guard House, Tiffany Turtle shines like a diadem. A stained-glass jewel in Tybee's crown, she sparkles like a pirate's chest, full of rubies and emeralds.

She's symbolic of more treasure soon to be buried on Tybee's beaches. Loggerhead sea turtle nesting season begins May 1, and on dark nights females will drag themselves up to the dune line to dig holes, lay their eggs, and bury them in the sands where they themselves were born.

The nests will be protected and cared for by volunteers with the Tybee Sea Turtle Project, headed by Tammy Smith. She is a teacher at the Tybee Island Maritime Academy, and her students reap the benefits of her commitment. And of the ocean being their backyard.

Principal Patrick Rossiter calculates that, as the seagull flies, it was 400 yards from their classroom to the nest Ms. Smith took them to last September. They witnessed her excavate the nest for stragglers. They recorded in their notebooks data on the live hatchlings, ones that did not survive, the number of hatched and unhatched eggs. Then they got to see the maiden swims of the 12 exuberant newborn turtles as they scrambled into the surf.

Mr. Rossiter says that field trip is an example of the research project-based approach the charter school uses – with students sketching cross-sections of the nest, describing the shore contours, the sand texture, the tidal parameters, and understanding the DNA testing of an egg from each nest by the State.

The K-4 school with 150 students is growing next year to a K-5 with 250 students. The school's success reads like the Holy Trinity of classic New Orleans recipes: students interested in learning, motivated teachers willing to try novel ideas, and committed parents.

I met some of Ms. Smith's students last week in front of City Hall, appreciating another of Tybee's public-art loggerheads. Turtle Vision by Sally Bostwick is covered with scenes familiar to all Tybee residents. The Cockspur Island lighthouse, schools of mullet, horseshoe crabs, blue crabs, hermit crabs, sand dollars, sea gulls and pelicans, sheepshead nibbling on barnacles, diamondback terrapins, shrimp boats, dolphins, and fossil shark teeth.

She rests on a weathered driftwood pedestal, and with all her maritime totems, it is good luck to touch her head before going inside to address City Council.

Thanks to the Tybee Arts Association there are more of these big loggerheads around the island. Captain Jack by Nancy Easterlin stands before his ship's wheel at the Crab Shack. Terrapin Towers by Julie Lieberman is a sandcastle-bearing turtle that is the first exciting thing kids see as their parents check in at Tybee Beach Vacation Rentals.

He Ain't Heavy by Irene Sullivan swims at the entrance to the Y; clinging to his back is a waterlogged bunny rabbit who looks like he's exhausted after a long dive. At Memorial Park Terra Turtle by Linda Lindeborg carries the world on her back.

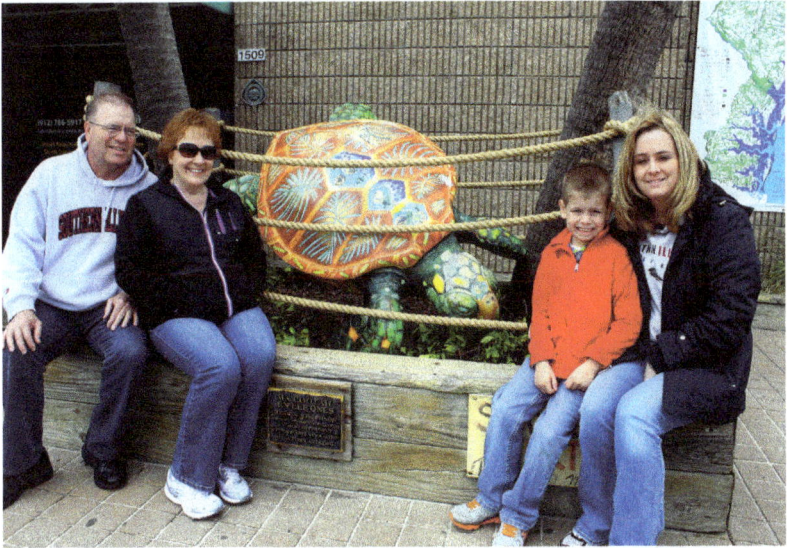

And in front of the Tybee Marine Science Center you will find Gullah-style Ma Cootah by Don Josephson, snacking on the vegetation between two palm trees.

Inside the Center swims a lucky little loggerhead named Ike. He was rescued last August when his nest was overrun by fire ants, but now he is on a full scholarship from the local Ikea Distribution Center. Hence his name.

Ikea is covering all of Ike's expenses, his care and feeding, and his regular wellness exams down at the Georgia Sea Turtle Center in Jekyll Island. Ikea has also sponsored Hodge Elementary this year to participate in the Center's Sidewalk to the Sea field trip program.

Around his birthday Ike will be carried out to the Gulf Stream and released. Until then he is the star of the Science Center's Facebook page, where his growth and every move are a delight to watch. Right now, at 8 months old, he weighs 1½ pounds.

Tomorrow morning (Saturday, April 26) a much bigger loggerhead will be released into the surf. Right after the 10th annual Tybee Turtle Trot.

The 5K beach run/walk takes place every year at the beginning of the loggerhead nesting season. Registration opens 7:30 at the Pavilion, and the trot begins at 8:30. It is the main fund-raiser for the Tybee Sea Turtle Project, which last year monitored 21 nests and 2092 eggs on the island. So every runner counts in the effort to save this threatened species.

The 96-pound turtle named Apex had a nasty encounter with a shark last July. He was found stranded, with bite marks on his badly crushed carapace, and his left front flipper was partially bitten off.

But Apex has been rehabilitated by the biologists at Jekyll and is healed and ready to take to the ocean again. He is being driven up tomorrow morning for his release. And by evening he might be all the way out to the Sargasso Sea.

From Tybee sand, Artist Mary Ingalls fired the glass for Tiffany Turtle in her home kiln. Soon, under the watchful eyes of dedicated volunteers, other little living gems will be incubated in loggerhead nests on our warm beaches.

Coming home from the Easter sunrise service last Sunday, North Beach residents said that Tiffany Turtle looked brighter than usual. Like a Faberge egg. I think that's a good sign.

10

A 500-Year-Old Tar Baby

Unique stamped tar wheels found in the shadow of the Tybee Lighthouse may be clues to early Spanish exploration. Historians puzzle over these links from Columbus and Trinidad to Tybee.

10

A 500-Year-Old Tar Baby

Do you remember the Uncle Remus story about Brer Rabbit and his misadventures with the silent Tar Baby? One after another the hands and feet of the aggravated Brer Rabbit got hopelessly stuck. Until he tricked Brer Fox into getting him loose.

Since 2006 Tybee Island resident Frank Drudi has been captivated by a different sort of Tar Baby. One that is 500 years old and came from Trinidad.

When Frank's neighbor was digging a swimming pool, Frank said that he could put the sand from the hole onto his empty lot. When the sand was spread, he found three heavy rough discs, clearly man-made. On the edge of each was an impressed seal that Frank recognized as a Spanish Cross.

That started the research wheels turning. What were these artifacts, dug up barely a hundred yards from the Tybee lighthouse? And what clues did the four letters S-O-C-G in the quadrants around the cross provide?

Daniel Elliott of the Lamar Institute performed an exhaustive archaeological survey of Frank's lot, now described as the Drudi tract. He used ground-penetrating radar and systematic sampling to look at Frank's property, but nothing else turned up.

Frank discovered that the discs were made of tar that Spanish mariners of the sixteenth century used to seal leaks in their ships' hulls. Tar that came from a huge pitch lake at La Brea, Trinidad, discovered by Columbus in 1498.

From poring over history books and talking to experts on early Spanish exploration of the Southeast coast, Frank has arrived at a persuasive theory of when and how the tar objects came to Tybee.

In 1521 two navigators sailing together out of the Caribbean, under contract to different aristocrats, both claimed land surrounding Winyah Sound near Georgetown, SC. Claiming land, for the crown and the sponsor, involved performing a standard ceremonial ritual and recording the event by ship's notary. A legal dispute followed over who had rights to explore and settle the vast coastal area. The king of Spain, Charles of Ghent, decided in favor of Luis Vasquez de Ayllon, whose captain had performed the ritual hours ahead of the other claimant.

Having the authority to explore this barely-charted coast, in 1525 Ayllon sent Pedro de Quejo to do further reconnaissance and double-check the desirability of Winyah Bay for settlement. Taking no chances on establishing claims this time, Ayllon instructed Quejo to place stone markers with the king's name and the date.

Not a single one of those stone markers has been found. But according to Quejo's logs his first stop was at latitude 32.0 degrees. Sound familiar? That's Tybee. This means that on May 3, 1525, the first Europeans to set foot on Georgia soil did it on Tybee sand. And the river that Quejo named the Rio de la Cruz on that date is the Savannah River.

Frank figures that, when no stones were around to erect as markers, Quejo formed markers of his own. A composite of sand, grass, and the caulking tar he had on board. And what more natural point for the claim than the location that was later chosen in Oglethorpe's day for the lighthouse?

In July 1526 Ayllon set sail from Hispaniola with six ships and 600 settlers straight to Winyah Bay. But the mother ship foundered on a sand bar before landing. Many supplies were lost; the area was not as suitable for agriculture as described; there were too few Native Americans with whom to work and trade. So Ayllon improvised a Plan B.

His expedition sailed south searching for a better location. On September 29, 1526, they established the settlement of San Miguel de Gualdape. Somewhere along the Georgia coast, maybe on Sapelo Sound. Named perhaps for the Guale Indians of the area. Ayllon himself died of illness there; the colony lasted about six weeks before the survivors sailed home; and its site has never been found.

Maybe Frank Drudi's markers hold a clue. Frank has looked long and hard at these tar babies, trying to coax more answers from them. But like Brer Rabbit, now he's a bit stuck.

When he heard about the West Chatham Middle School students who were studying early Spanish missions along the Georgia coast, he decided

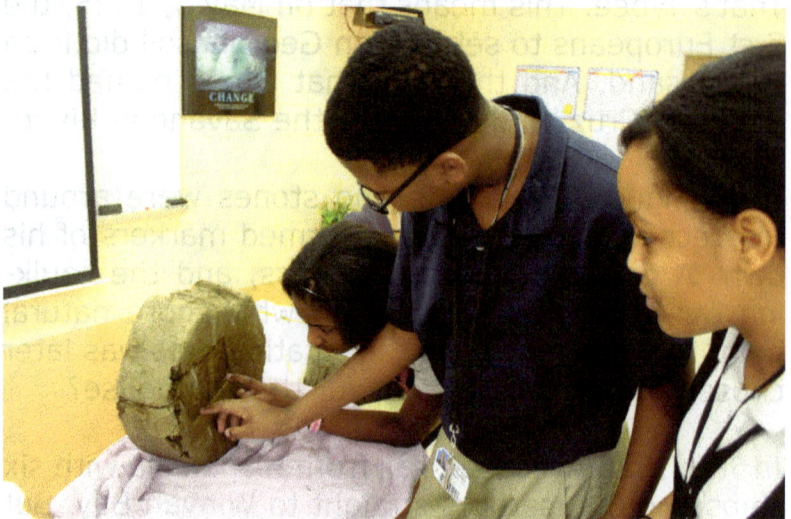

to see if their young minds could bring new eyes and ideas to answer some of his questions. Why haven't more of these tar objects been discovered elsewhere? What do the letters S-O-C-G mean?

Frank deputized me to carry the tar markers, almost 60 pounds each, like they were Faberge eggs, to show to the students. It was a good move. The students and their teachers Mrs. Jacquelin Harden and Mr. Josh Wonders were very interested to see these old relics that are, so far, one-of-a-kind.

And they offered fresh insights. Samantha Jenkins suggested searching for references to "rough asphalt cylinders" in explorers' narratives and that the letters may be initials for a church. Francheska Gonzalez suggested that there are more and larger markers nearby and always on the southern shores of their rivers.

Several of the students speak Spanish, so may discover Spanish-language journals, diaries, or records that refer to the markers or the voyages. Regan Gayadeen said that she has family in Trinidad and would get them involved to look for similar tar objects in museums and collections around La Brea.

Diamond Folston and Sade Baker had experience making charcoal rubbings of cemetery headstones, so they took rubbings of the Spanish crosses to study more closely. Jack Steuwe commented on the markers' plasticity, and Nicholas Bergeron on their symbolism.

Some students were intrigued whether the seals stamped in the markers were made ahead of time in Hispaniola or on board the ships as situations changed. All three of the Drudi objects have the same imprint, but in other locations might different letters be used? And maybe we should search for the wooden stampers that were carved to impress the seals; like searching for the branding iron and not the brand.

Could the markers have been moved at all by Indians? Are the letters really S-O-C-G, or are they D-O-C-G? Does C-G stand for Carlos de Gante (King Charles of Ghent) as Frank assumes or for something else? Could the G stand for Gualdape? The S for San or Santa?

Students Cameron Myers, John Winters, and John Tyner lingered to look at the markers from all sides. They pointed out the wood impressions on the undersides and holes that might have been for lifting them. They suggested X-raying the markers to see if they contained medals or coins put in by the seamen who fabricated them.

They suggested that 3-D scans be made of the markers, so that they could be 3-D printed and examined by other researchers. And that with high definition perhaps the wood grain and grass imprints might help tell the story.

Tybee DPW Superintendent Danny Carpenter is equally fascinated. He has found hundreds of artifacts from the Civil War, the Fort Screven era, and

even from the lost Martello Tower. He says, "These tar markers are a Tybee mystery, like the Tybee Bomb. But I think they are far more significant."

He and Frank are hopeful that the West Chatham students make a break-through, crack this DaVinci code, and get the tar babies to reveal their secrets.

11

A Shrimp Boat's History

Docked at Lazaretto Creek is a shrimp boat that has had only two captains in her long life. The Agnes Marie holds a sacred spot in many a Tybee heart.

11

A Shrimp Boat's History

Folks from Savannah and Tybee Island know that there is a magic you feel as you pass over the Lazaretto Creek Bridge. It's like you're a seagull gliding home, warmed by the light on the water below.

From the top of the bridge, you see on your left the little Cockspur Island lighthouse, its weathered white stone a connection to history and a million tides. And beyond it lies the vast expanse of the Savannah River and the low country of South Carolina.

Below on your right are the docks that are home to Tybee's crabbers, charter fishermen, and shrimpers. And there is one shrimp boat moored there that seems to meet your gaze and whisper a welcome home. She's the Agnes Marie, and her captain, J.B. Riffle has a story you will not forget.

J.B. rode across that bridge on a Harley over for-ty years ago. "I was a young man, with long hair, a messy beard, and fifty dollars in my pocket. I needed a fresh start.

"And I got it from Captain William Glenn Smith. W.G. saw something in me that I didn't even see myself. I went to work for him on the Carol Ann, named for his granddaughter.

"W.G. said that I was born for shrimping. On deck, I could head and sort 900 pounds a day. W.G. taught me how to weld, to work on the engines, to mend nets.

"I was there in Shallotte, N.C. in 1978 when the Agnes Marie was built. W.G. named her for his wife and daughter.

"She's a wooden boat, with white cedar ribs, deck planks of tongue-and-groove pine, and cypress sheathing for the hull. W.G. always said that a steel

boat sits in the water. A fiberglass boat sits on the water. But a wooden boat sits with the water."

J.B. says that Captain W.G. became like a father to him and set a good example in many ways. He refused offers to run drugs. He refused to profit from the Mariel boatlift. He paid his crew honestly for their hard work.

When it came time to retire from shrimping, W.G. sold the Agnes Marie to J.B. "as long as you promise to let me work on her until I die." And the new captain kept that promise.

"W.G. tried retirement for a while after I bought the boat, but he was part of the sea and wanted to come back to work. It was his home. It was his life.

"He got very ill over his last five years and was not able-bodied, but I let him work on the boat all those years, for a full crew share, so that he would feel needed and that he was earning his way.

"I knew how to drive the boat like he taught me, so I let him take the wheel and work his favorite grounds. He was at the wheel the day he passed away.

"It was the morning of Veterans Day 2006; I was beside him when he simply released the wheel and slumped to the floor. We were crossing the Savannah River channel. We hadn't set out our nets yet, and we had been saying what a good day we had yesterday.

"It was just past low tide, and we were heading North by Northeast, toward Calibogue."

That's where we went last Friday morning, the day after Thanksgiving. I went along with Capt. J.B. and his striker John-Boy Solomon on their first trip with the engines under load. They had rebuilt the engines the previous week and had to wait out wind advisories for several days.

In fifteen feet of water off Daufuskie Island, J.B. watched his chart to avoid all the X's that marked hangs. They pulled in their small try net to get a preview of the catch; it looked good, with glistening white shrimp and little unwanted or troublesome by-catch.

After a two-hour drag, they hauled in the nets, one on each outrigger, and hundreds of seagulls and pelicans swarmed to the boat, perching on the nets while still in the water. J.B. and John-Boy winched the bags onto the boat and emptied out over 200 pounds of beautiful shrimp.

I was amazed at the ongoing battle to keep the seagulls away from the catch; they constantly

snatched shrimp from the edges of the pile. And swallowed fish a third their size.

John-Boy culled out the shrimp, keeping the blue crabs and whiting in separate baskets, and pushing overboard numerous small horseshoe crabs, hog choker flounders, some spot, and several stingrays. J.B. works like W.G. before him, doing everything for the quality of the shrimp. He ices them down in coolers rather than letting them sit in the hold. He uses bigger mesh to avoid catching small shrimp. He drags shorter so that the catch is not crushed in the bags.

The old Williams Seafood used to get their shrimp entirely from W.G. and then J.B. On our way back to the dock, J.B. was getting calls from Tybee's best restaurants, placing orders for the day's catch. Those shrimp were destined for Gerald's Pig and Shrimp, A-J's Dockside, Sting Ray's, the Breakfast Club. And of course the Sundae Café, where a large photo of the Agnes Marie at sunset fills an entire wall.

J.B. called W.G.'s old friend Deacon Nathaniel Smith of the Faith Gospel Temple Deliverance Center in Port Wentworth. He was giving them the two dozen blue crabs and the two-dozen nice whiting. "All I ever ask is for them to just pray for me." J.B. routinely drops off free shrimp to older women on fixed incomes. And he charges $1 a pound to needy folks who insist he take some payment.

"I'm blessed to work these waters. I was blessed to feel like W.G.'s son. W.G. wasn't a religious man, but he was spiritual. I've become both.

"When we got back to the dock that day in 2006, my own son Josiah met us. I tried to pick W.G. up; I wanted to carry him off the boat, but I wasn't strong enough. I broke down, and then Josiah put his hand on my shoulder and said, 'Daddy, I got him.'

"I felt like, with that effort, my own son became a man that day, a final gift from W.G. I had kissed W.G. on the forehead when he first fell to the floor, and I kissed him again after Josiah laid him on the gurney."

The Agnes Marie still lives. Moored in W.G.'s same spot at the dock. And in Bonaventure Cemetery, William Glenn Smith rests beside his wife Agnes, with a shrimp boat etched on their headstone.

Their graves are near the bluff along the Wilmington River. From there you can see the shrimp boats from Thunderbolt heading toward Carolina. And as they pass Bonaventure, they are heading North by Northeast.

12

Loving the Live Bottom

Gray's Reef is one of only fourteen National Marine Sanctuaries. It lies 19 miles off the coast below beautiful blue water and is a manta ray mecca.

12

Loving the Live Bottom

Georgia Southern Biology professor Dr. Danny Gleason has spent a lot of time crawling over the live bottom of Gray's Reef. He is a marine invertebrate guy, who studies sponges, corals, and sea squirts, but his most awe-inspiring experience involved a startling encounter with a big fish.

A dozen years ago, diving with a group of his graduate students, his field of vision suddenly dimmed as he found himself under a sprawling shadow. And as he felt something rest lightly on his head and shoulders like a broad carpet.

It was sort of a flying carpet - a giant oceanic Manta Ray with a 10-foot wingspan. "I pushed it away, but it came up against me again. I realized that it hadn't bumped against me accidentally but wanted my attention. It raised its fins and arched back in a way that let me know it wanted me to scratch its belly. So that's what I did."

Dr. Gleason looked around and saw that some smaller 4-to-5-foot mantas had made their own contact with his students and had coaxed them into scratching their undersides too. "They were using us like cleaning stations, maybe rubbing off some miniscule parasites. They hung around for a few days. It was hard to get anything else done because they kept demanding our attention, and we were glad to give it. None of us will ever forget the sight of those giants gliding so gracefully over the reef."

Experiences at Gray's Reef seem to burn into your memory. Just 19 miles east of Sapelo Island, in 60-70 feet of water, it is part of an elite group of only 14 National Marine Sanctuaries. They stretch from sea to shining sea, but Gray's Reef is the only one of these protected treasures on the Georgia continental shelf. It is 22 square miles, roughly the shape of an emerald-cut diamond.

Cathy Sakas was the Education Coordinator at Gray's Reef for 15 years. "I remember the first time I saw it. The day was calm; the water was glassy with not a ripple; it was a pure green that meant it was rich with phytoplankton.

"Ahead of us I could see a commotion of birds, and I knew they were over the reef. Hundreds of shearwaters and petrels skimming the surface. Sleek gannets climbing a hundred feet, diving, and spearing the water in pursuit of little scad and squid.

"And then I saw the bobbing russet-brown carapaces of several loggerhead sea turtles. They were not bothered by us, but swam leisurely away, raising their big heads to look at us over their shoulders."

Down below is the hard bottom, the sandstone out-croppings that protrude from the sandy seafloor. They were formed millions of years ago from ce-mented terrestrial and marine sediments. And be-tween 40,000 and 10,000 years ago, when sea lev-el was lower and the shoreline was 80 miles east of where it is today, Gray's Reef was dry land.

So it is that geologists have found there fossils and bones of bison, camels, ground sloths, mastodons, and woolly mammoths. And seeds and spores of an evergreen fir forest. Hand-tooled deer antlers uncovered there were likely fashioned as spear tips by Timucuan Indians 15,000 years ago.

Now these long-submerged rocky ledges, caves, crevices, and crannies are perfect terrain for in-vertebrates to attach. And among those sponges, corals, barnacles, and hard-tubed worms, all sorts of crabs, fish, and organisms thrive.

On a night dive in a one-man submersible, Sakas cut the engine and lights and rested the sub on the reef floor. As her eyes adjusted to the darkness, she was dazzled by the scores of comb jellies that luminesced as they bumped against the observation dome. Every crevice seemed to twinkle with light, like homes of a Lilliputian village. Over several vertical feet iridescent green light appeared in bands every few inches, waving in the current.

Sakas and over 60 other marine sanctuary educators and scientists were trained on the submersibles under the Sustainable Seas Expeditions program, the brainchild of Dr. Sylvia Earle. National Geographic Explorer-in-Residence and oceanographic superstar, Earle is the headliner for the Ocean Film Festival that runs tonight and tomorrow at the Lucas Theater.

There is serious depth to this Festival. Dr. Earle is referred to around the globe as "Her Deepness."

She holds the world record for the deepest solo dive without a tether. She will speak tonight after her film "Mission Blue."

James Cameron, of "Titanic" fame, set the record for the first solo submarine dive to the deepest place on Earth, the Mariana Trench. The film about the feat "Deep Sea Challenge" shows tomorrow night, and its director will speak afterward.

The Gray's Reef National Marine Sanctuary Foundation (graysreefnmsf.org) just launched in November. Its mission is to protect and support the sanctuary and to spread the good news about oceans and sea life.

This film festival is a great start, with inspiring films for children and adults. Their website goes into more depth about their vision and invites children to become involved at the "Sea Star" level with a small donation.

Gray's Reef Sanctuary Superintendent Sarah Fangman is delighted that the Foundation has formed. "Their support will help us promote the sanctuary for research, education, recreational diving and fishing.

"We have a fascinating acoustic fish tagging study. We have transmitting microchips in black sea bass, gag groupers, red snappers, and scamp groupers, so we are able to track their movement and behavior. And the amazing thing is that we have discovered that Atlantic Sturgeon microchipped in New York visit the reef. And we've picked up Great White Sharks microchipped in New England.

"Temperate and tropical waters intersect here, so we have very interesting seasonal visitors. Bull and lemon sharks come up from Florida. Mackerel, barracuda, and jacks abound at different times.

"The reef is dynamic. You can watch little cubbyu grow from gangly juveniles to sleek adults from spring to summer. We have gorgeous butterflyfish, wrasses, eels, puffers, and angelfish, all against brilliantly colored sponges and corals.

"We were the third designated marine sanctuary, in 1981 by President Carter. We want the people of Georgia to enjoy it and learn about it. It's their sanctuary."

After I spoke with Fangman, I spent so much time on their website (graysreef.noaa.gov) that I almost got the bends. Of course, I asked her about manta rays. She said that she has seen them numerous times and that they are magical to watch; they look like they are flying and have hovered above her on dives. They seem to like the exhaust bubbles tickling their bellies like a Jacuzzi.

Former Research Coordinator Greg McFall said that he once had a 7-foot manta light on his head. It had a large remora attached that it wanted McFall to dislodge. As he brushed the remora away, the manta immediately sped off, with the remora, after it got its bearings, in hot pursuit.

Mantastic. I joined the Gray's Reef National Marine Sanctuary Foundation and feel more buoyant already. It's an obvious way, in my mind's eye, to reach out and scratch the belly of a ray.

13

Surrounded by Dolphins

Bottlenose dolphins thrive along the shores of Tybee and in the tidal creeks. What they eat, where they sleep, and what they dream are news to use.

13

Surrounded by Dolphins

In Hemingway's The Old Man and the Sea, at the end of a grueling day, the old fisherman Santiago lay exhausted in his small boat. During the night, alone in the Gulf Stream, he was consoled by the sounds of dolphins. "He could tell the difference between the blowing noise the male made and the sighing blow of the female."

One chilly morning last month I rode along with Savannah State researchers on the Tiger II, as they looked for common bottlenose dolphins in the Herb and Wilmington Rivers. You could hear the sharp exhales of the ones we spotted. And in the cool marsh air you could see their breaths frost up in foggy plumes.

At the wheel was Dr. Tara Cox, head of SSU's Dolphin Studies Program. It's a powerhouse of a program, with two graduate and eleven Marine Science undergraduate students currently involved. They survey the estuarine area from the Savannah River to Ossabaw Sound year-round, doing at least two surveys a month fall to spring, and at least ten a month in summer.

Their goal is to get the most complete picture possible of the dolphins that cruise our rivers, creeks, and sounds. They take dorsal fin photos of every dolphin spotted; those fins are as unique as human fingerprints and serve to identify each individual.

Dr. Cox and her team were featured in the Georgia Outdoors episode "Dolphin Drama" that aired on GPB a year ago. It turns out that our Savannah dolphins break the world records for begging. By a lot.

Dolphins that approach humans, looking to be fed, are more susceptible to propeller strikes, fishing gear entanglement, and lower reproductive success. It's been illegal to feed dolphins for about 20 years, but begging is a hard habit to extinguish.

Sometimes there are especially tragic consequences, like the case of a calf nicknamed Fall. When researchers first saw the youngster in 2009, he already had a mangled fluke and a healed shark bite. His mother Summer was a non-stop beggar at the Lazaretto shrimp boat dock. Two months after shrimping season ended, he was found dead on the beach, malnourished, emaciated, and with additional shark wounds. His mother had taught him to be too dependent on well-meaning humans for food.

A healthy mother-calf bond is critical. Dolphins have signature whistles, and the calf learns his mother's immediately. He develops his own in about a month; it's effectively his name, and dolphins call each other's signature whistles like kids at a soccer game.

A newborn, until he builds up buoyant blubber and can swim independently, is carried along in his mother's slipstream. The mother teaches the calf survival skills; she will injure fish to make them easy for the calf to catch. Through echolocation, dolphins can find schools of fish and even distinguish what species they are.

They are social animals and readily pick up skills from each other. A behavior called "strand feeding" is only seen in Low-Country dolphins. A group will herd fish onto a mud bank and throw themselves up on the bank as well, always on their right sides, and eat the fish on that side of their mouths.

Those right-side teeth are worn down by the grit in the mud. The group, lying together on a bank, like fingers of a big glove, eat the stranded fish, then wiggle their way into the water to do it again. And mothers have been seen teaching calves how to do it, but on steeper banks, so there is no chance of stranding while training.

In population studies, a dolphin is usually just a number. But when the SSU team gets hands-on, it's natural to name the dolphin. In 2008 citizen volunteers with Savannah's Dolphin Project reported a dolphin in distress; he had a thick rubber ring around his neck that would eventually strangle him. He proved to be very hard to find, earning him the nickname Waldo. After days of searching, Dr. Cox's team finally found the dolphin and cut loose the ring. She turned out to be a female, but by then the name had stuck. The scar around her neck still shows, but she is alive and well, photographed just last month.

The SSU team has focused on human-dolphin interaction, with an eye toward helping dolphins make the right lifestyle changes. Researcher Carolyn Kovacs spent two summers on the Tybee shrimp boat Agnes Marie, quantifying dolphin behavior during trawling. Based on her work and their own observation, to combat begging, shrimpers make every effort to push bycatch overboard in open water instead of near their docks.

Capt. J.B. Riffle has seen some of the same dolphins for forty years. They will come alongside, fish or no fish, to look you in the eye. "Some of them grew up with my son Josiah. When he was a boy, they'd jump up to touch his outstretched hand. They recognize him still whenever he's on board. I think they know he's a good soul.

"Dolphins won't eat what's not good for them. They'll spit out catfish. They really aren't very fond of shrimp. But they go wild over ribbon fish. And they'll toss jelly balls back and forth for sport."

Only once, in the days before nets had turtle excluders, did J.B. ever catch a dolphin. It was a short drag on the Daufuskie breakers. As they were bringing in the net, they were shocked to see two large dolphins in its throat. And then they saw why.

In the bag of the net was a dolphin calf, maybe 3 feet long and 100 pounds. The adults had gone in to help him. J.B. could see that he was still alive.

There were about 150 pounds of shrimp in the bag, but J.B. had no intention of dumping the bag onto the deck and hurting the calf. He took both engines out of gear to stop the propellers.

They brought the bag alongside and opened it as close to the water as they could, so the calf would not drop very far. It made a bee line over to the adults who were still in the net. They winched the net up to slide the adults out the mouth.

"That calf couldn't stop jumping. I smile whenever I think of how we saved the little guy."

Allen Lewis, who has been a captain for Capt. Mike's Dolphin Tours for six years, says, "The reward of our job is smiles. We are blessed to have so many dolphins around Tybee. I think that there are maybe 40 year-round residents and hundreds in summer when the bait fish show up.

"People get to see the dolphins feeding, along the sandbars or jetties. Working as teams, tossing menhaden or mackerel high in the air and throwing stingrays like Frisbees.

"We'll point out neonates with their fetal folds. Or dark newborns swimming in their mothers' shadows. We'll point out nursery areas in some quiet shallows.

"Occasionally I'll point out dolphins sleeping. They have to breathe deliberately, so they can't go totally asleep. They rest one brain hemisphere at a time and keep one eye open.

"Our tours are by the book. Because we like the book. We don't disrupt any normal dolphin activities. Our dream is to be the first operation in the Southeast to be certified by NOAA's Dolphin Smart program this year."

Later in Hemingway's tale, old Santiago had a dream of miles of dolphins leaping in the air. Two years ago French scientists recorded captive dolphins talking in their sleep. They were not talking dolphin. They were talking humpback whale. They were captive-bred dolphins who had never heard humpbacks in the wild, but they discerned their songs in the background soundtrack at the dolphinarium.

What do they dream of here? Right whales? The lighthouse? The Agnes Marie?

14

Tybee's Little White House

From 1897 to 1945 Tybee's Fort Screven was home to famous soldiers. A century plant towers over a building unchanged since its days as the Post's commo hut.

14

Tybee's Little White House

This summer I've sipped iced tea on the back porch at the White House a few times. And gotten a walk around the grounds with the First Lady. All without leaving Tybee Island.

I don't mean a virtual tour; I mean the real thing. Just down Second Avenue from the Sugar Shack are the old sentry post pillars that marked the eastern entrance to Fort Screven. And just beyond them lies the most unassuming little white bungalow, snug and quiet on a vast lot.

It is named "The White House," after Tom and Louise White who bought it in 1960. It was built in 1897 and served as the communications building for the Fort. "We kept it as it was, never remodeled or rented it out. We added the porch, that's all."

Mrs. White recalls how years ago a long-haired, long-bearded old seaman pulled up to the house in a beat-up old truck and asked if he could look inside. He had been stationed at Fort Screven during WWI. Stepping inside the house, into a room instantly familiar, brought back memories of many happy nights playing poker with his buddies around the fuel-oil heater, their backs to the switchboard in the radio shack.

The house sits comfortably in its own skin, a witness to years of history. In 1932 Lt. Col. George Marshall came to Fort Screven on his first command. He loved the island and is responsible for planting many of the crepe myrtle trees that still adorn Jaycee Park and other byways of the old post.

His morning routine involved riding around the Fort on his horse Applejack, for fresh air and to inspect the grounds. You can just envision the horse tethered to the railings that still lead to the White House front door.

After WWII Fort Screven was decommissioned, the property passed to the city, and the little communications building at the gates to the Fort came to have a connection to Savannah's Bethesda Home for Boys. Elizabeth Johnson, a beloved Bethesda teacher for fifty years, bought it for her retirement.

She sold it to Tom and Louise in 1960. Tom was a Bethesda boy. He had been raised at the orphanage. Its influence and the lessons he learned there were a constant for his entire life.

He had a deep love for the Home and for all his classmates. He became a Presbyterian minister, serving first in Savannah, and ultimately for fifty years in Covington until his passing in 1997.

Louise says that the boys at Bethesda were his family. "They loved each other. They kept up with each other. Tom was called back many times to marry boys he had gone to school with."

He was asked to bury faculty who had taught him, and he considered performing those funerals the highest honor. He was especially touched to be asked to conduct the service for Ole W. Burroughs, who had been the Director of Bethesda while Tom grew up there.

Louise grew up on Ferguson Avenue near Bethesda, and breezes from Moon River blew her way too. Johnny Mercer's aunt Ann Rivers was her neighbor and had a profound influence on her life.

She was a nurse, and that is what led Louise to enter and graduate from the Candler Hospital School of Nursing. And seemingly minor memories of long ago have a way of still coming into play.

Louise's small utility building has a sign on it identifying it as "The Capsule." It sits on the foundation of what was a sentry tower in General Marshall's day. I thought that its name must have a military significance.

But that's not the case. "Ann Rivers called her guest house 'the capsule.' I don't know why. But when we built the shed, we called it that too, because I remember how I felt about my old neighbor, my old friend."

Some things you just can't predict. Like when a century plant will bloom. In 1960, when they bought the house, a friend gave Louise a century plant because she has always loved cactuses.

Prickly pears, yuccas, and century plants do well in Tybee's arid sands. Louise has planted others, but that original century plant has weathered 55 years just off the porch and has been something of the botanical patriarch of the White House.

Century plants are agaves and look fearsome with their thick sword-like leaves with sharp tips and saw-tooth edges. But one day, one year, they do what most plants do – they flower, and they do it mightily.

This summer Louise's has bloomed. Who knows what makes a century plant stir and decide that this is the season, but almost overnight it sends a stalk skyward at breakneck speed. Where there was the tough gray-green rosette, suddenly something that looks like a giant asparagus has shot up.

Most plants reach to the sky, but there is an exuberance and energy that is special about the way a century plant does it. Like the cry of a prophet in the desert, it announces its presence and carries a message.

This one next to the White House now hovers 23 feet. Taller than the chimney. As tall as the sentry tower that stood above "The Capsule."

A century plant only flowers once and then it dies. The shaft that bears the flowers shoots up like a periscope, to see and be seen. What is it seeking at those heights?

It is as though the plant has a need to reach a height where birds and butterflies and bats can find it, where the first rays of the sun can catch it, where its saffron blooms can announce that it has lived.

There is tranquility to the White House. It's always been a place for people driving past to slow and rest their eyes. And this year, like a healing pool at Bethesda, a century plant reaching to heaven marks it as more special yet.

15

Squirming Diamondbacks

Diamondback terrapins love the salt marsh and tidal creeks. Students watch and learn as young terrapins are released to the wild, destined to dodge predators and motorists.

15

Squirming Diamondbacks

The school year has just begun, but three Diamond-back Terrapins just graduated from Head Start. On Sept. 10 third-grade students from Thunderbolt Elementary came to Fort Pulaski to see the terrapins swim off into the great big world.

It was all under the watchful eyes of Tybee Island Marine Science Center staff who have cared for the terrapins since they were brought to the Center as rescued hatchlings in spring of 2013. Then they were barely the size of quarters but are now hefty two-year-olds about the size of a fist.

And it was only right that students from Thunderbolt were the cheerleaders for the three terrapins because the school mascot is the turtle. The outdoor walkways around the school are full of stenciled sea turtles.

Another connection to Thunderbolt was the name of one of the terrapins – Tubby. He was found by an employee of Tubby's Tank House in a dangerous location for a baby terrapin, the restaurant parking lot.

The other two terrapins, found by lifeguards on Tybee's north beach, were named Pearl and Runt. Pearl got her name from her creamy, blond shell that seems to glow. Runt got his name from his small size, but he was as healthy and strong as Tubby and Pearl.

Diamondback terrapins are a threatened species in Georgia and are most vulnerable when young, to predation by birds, raccoons, large fish, and snakes. Curator Chantal Audran of the Marine Science Center said that the program is called Head Start because it gives the terrapins some age and strength to improve their odds of survival.

During their two years at the Center Tubby, Pearl, and Runt were fed a terrapin pellet diet. But in the weeks before their release they were introduced to fiddler crabs, which are a big part of their natural diet. Audran said that all three recognized the fiddlers right away as food and chased them around with no hesitation.

She pointed out to the children that there were plenty of fiddler crabs in the marsh where the terrapins were being released, just over the Fort Pulaski bridge in a protected area with little boat traffic.

The Thunderbolt students were there as participants in the Center's Sidewalk to the Sea Program which connects city kids with coastal and offshore environments. As they poured off their bus, Audran recognized a lot of the children who have been coming to Sidewalk since kindergarten.

The children got introduced to Tubby, Pearl, and Runt and saw how each was marked in a unique way so that scientists could tell who was who if they are recaptured in the future. Audran had used a small triangular file to put notches in five of the peripheral scutes of their shells.

Terrapins have 24 of these scutes, identified as A through X clockwise around the edge of the shell. Georgia DNR gave the codes to Audran and has in their database now Runt (Mr. CMNQW), Tubby (Mr. CMNQX), and Pearl (Miss CMNVW).

The students formed a double line, and all got to touch the terrapins as Audran and Marine Science Educator Alli Williford carried them down the marsh bank to the water's edge. All those pats on the back, the laying on of all those third-grade hands, certainly helped add promise to this first day on their own for three young terrapins.

The students then lined up along the bank to watch the release. And, on three, cheered "Good Luck." They were excited to see the little heads and noses poke out of the water. And they were able to recognize each terrapin and cheer them on.

Pearl and Tubby came right back to shore, and Audran took them down to a grassier area where they were more comfortable. One little boy wanted to swim out in the creek to show them how to do it.

When the three terrapins were all safe and adjusted to their new environment, the students departed, saying, "Good luck, Pearl," "We love you, Tubby," and "Keep swimming, Runt." One of the Thunderbolt teachers called out, "Run, Forrest, run." That can't hurt.

The students continued onto Fort Pulaski and spent time in the maritime forest and marsh. They learned about the animals and plants that make the salt marsh such an enormous nursery for marine life.

Communications Director Cody Shelley says the Sidewalk to the Sea program is designed to be a continuum, building a sense of stewardship in the children. In three-hour field trips, kindergarteners get their feet wet learning about beach wildlife. First-graders strain animals from tidepools. Second-graders handle jellyfish.

Third-graders study terrapins and periwinkles. Fourth-graders examine animals living under floating docks. Fifth-graders dissect squids. Sixth-graders travel from Bull River, up the Savannah River to the Houlihan Bridge on the Center's floating classroom.

Shelley says, "It almost doesn't matter what we teach; the kids love getting up close with nature. We're hard-wired to love the sea."

She says that the kids' natural exuberance makes them soak up instruction like sponges. Beach walks and sunshine let them know that this is their coast. Shelley recalls one little boy from Savannah who, having never seen the ocean, marveled and asked in disbelief, "This is free?"

I spoke with Thunderbolt teacher Emily Morgan last week, and she said that the kids look forward to their Sidewalk to the Sea trip every year. "For some students it's their first time being near wildlife."

She mentioned one usually reserved student who was exuberant and answered question after question as Educator Joy Davis walked them down Pulaski's trails to the marsh. And back at school, they made some cross-curricular connections. One girl related the terrapins gaining their freedom to what they were covering in Social Studies - Paul Revere and freedom from taxes.

And observations about how Pearl kept turning back led to talk about social skills and occasions where hesitation is normal, like getting on a roller coaster or going to a new school.

I visited teacher April McMillians's class, and her students were eager to talk about Spartina marsh grass and predators and prey. They also made observations about how Runt turned out to be the bravest of the three terrapins, not swimming right back to shore. So sometimes you can't judge an animal or a person by appearances only.

McMillian said that they had related the terrapins, finding their way in the world with no mother to

guide them, to Opal, the heroine of Because of Winn Dixie, the book they are now reading. A girl Opal, a terrapin Pearl, it's a nice connection.

The 2016 class of Head Start hatchlings is on display in the Science Center aquariums. A total of 17 hatchlings from this year's turtle rescue.

Center staff monitor the number of terrapins that unfortunately get run over on the Tybee Road between Bull River and Lazaretto Creek during spring and summer. This year there were 119 casualties, mostly females crossing the road to lay eggs. But from those females they were able to extract 29 viable eggs which were successfully incubated by Dr. Kathryn Craven at AASU.

One girl in Ms. McMillian's class at Thunderbolt asked me, "Are terrapins intelligent?" I told her they were. Then she asked, "Are they trustworthy?" Yes, absolutely.

She said, "I'm going to tell my Daddy to be sure and slow down whenever we drive past Fort Pulaski." Slow down for Tubby. Slow down for Runt. Slow down for Pearl.

16

Seafood in Their Blood

The Ambos family of Thunderbolt is one of the areas most storied seafood families. The patriarch gets a surprise gift fit for an old shrimper.

16

Seafood in Their Blood

This summer I was invited along on a birthday road trip out of Tybee Island. Before dawn Capt. J.B. Riffle steered his shrimp boat, the Agnes Marie, under the graceful arch of the Lazaretto Creek bridge. Beside him sat Louis Ambos, in a wheelhouse for the first time in probably 30 years.

Ambos' eyes shined as he looked at the sun rising over the vast Atlantic. "There's the big red ball," he said to his wife Suzanne. "It peeks out at first, then seems to sit on the horizon, before it breaks free of a red cord connecting it to the water."

The Ambos family has been connected to these waters, to shrimping, and to Thunderbolt for over a hundred years. This excursion was all pleasure, set up by Ambos' sons Drew and Hal.

Last spring Drew had essentially been the location scout for a show in development for the Inspiration

channel. Hosted by Maureen McCormick, of Brady Bunch fame, and called "State Plate," it features foods from every state. The premier episode, to air in early 2016, features Georgia shrimp, fresh and wild-caught by the Agnes Marie.

After spending the filming day with J.B., Drew and Hal had a great idea. For his 76th birthday in July, they would take their father out on a working shrimp boat, like he had done when they were boys. With their mother, wives, and children on board too, they made it a family affair and a special present.

J.B. said that he was honored to have Louis on board. J.B.'s mentor W.G. Smith had sold his shrimp to Ambos Seafood years ago. W.G. had shrimped out of Thunderbolt, and he and his wife Agnes had lived on their boat, tied up to the Ambos docks.

That July day, shrimping in Calibogue Sound, was an inspired birthday gift. I could see that, for Louis, sitting in the captain's chair felt like going home.

Looking out of the wheelhouse windows, breathing the salt air, rocking on the open water, unlocked contentment and a lifetime of memories.

J.B. and Louis talked about outriggers and winches, nets and doors. But also about old-timers and old boats. A conversation between men with deep ties to these local creeks, rivers, and beaches.

On the wall of his office at Ambos Seafoods, Louis has a photo of his great-grandfather Henry and a treasured family document. It is the certificate from 1868 declaring that Henry, formerly "a subject of the King of Prussia," is granted US citizenship.

On another wall is an old lithograph of the Henry Ambos Restaurant in Thunderbolt. Circa 1870 there are no phone or power lines in the picture, just rowboats and skiffs at the restaurant dock, and advertisement of oysters, terrapin, etc.

Louis' grandfather (after whom he is named) was the first native of Thunderbolt to begin commercial

shrimping. He did that in 1927, the year Lindbergh crossed the Atlantic, and his first two boats were the Sweet Pickle and the Lindbergh.

He also operated a marine service railway, and during the off season he built homes along River Drive. Louis was born and raised in one of them – the restaurant section of what is now Tubby's Tank House. Now that is some provenance.

Louis' grandfather Louis and father Henry built a very successful fleet of shrimp boats during the 1930's and '40's. But in 1948 his father and Savannah grocer William Mullis made an advance that revolutionized the shrimping business.

Trade Winds' Thunderbolt, Ga., shrimp plant. The firms famed breaded fantail shrimp is among many items packed here.

After many recipe trials in their own kitchens, they developed battered, frozen shrimp that were pan-ready and could be shipped far and wide. Their company, Trade Winds, mushroomed in growth and by 1950 was distributing frozen oysters, scallops, and fish to all 48 states. The company created many factory jobs and put Thunderbolt on the national seafood map.

106

It's an Ambos way of life. You could say that Louis was there at the creation. His father took him and his twin brother Henry Jr. out in his boat while still in their cradles and crib.

Louis worked in the heading dock of Trade Winds at the age of ten, punching cards of workers to keep count of their buckets of headed shrimp. He remembers too going out with his grandfather on weekends to check his oyster beds.

He remembers the Greek boatwrights from Tarpon Springs trimming the ribs as they built the Miss Tradewinds. He showed me the scar on his ankle where he ran into one of their sharp axes.

Louis, his brother, and boyhood friends loved to ride the cradles of the marine railway, getting repeatedly baptized in the River Wilmington. And they dropped to the water from tire swings hanging from the davit cranes.

Those kinds of memories came back aboard the Agnes Marie. And talk of Thunderbolt friends like Anna Modestino and her restaurant, Anna's Little Napoli. Anna had earlier worked on Louis' father's shrimp breading line, and he loved Anna's hospitality, the intimate atmosphere, and her shrimp au gratin.

Louis talked about his father's deep friendship with Tassey Salas, who owned Tassey's Pier. He recalled many wonderful meals at Tassey's, especially the she-crab soup that made the pages of Esquire. Just yards away from Trade Winds, and overlooking the intracoastal, those crabs were not far from home.

Right now, for the Ambos family and seafood, it's five generations and counting. And the day aboard the Agnes Marie was one for the family album.

Each time the nets were drawn in, dolphins raced alongside, seagulls and pelicans balanced on the outriggers and cables. As the catch was dumped onto the deck, the kids were quick to go through it.

Drew's daughter Ashley and son Wynn were ready to pick up all the curiosities for his wife Liz to photograph: quarter-size horseshoe crabs, tiny triggerfish, silvery ribbonfish, glistening small pompano and Spanish mackerel. Hal's daughter Caroline chased his wife Nichole around with blue crabs, stingrays, and slender sharpnose sharks.

These kids, on a shrimp boat deck for the first time, were right at home. Ashley asked, "When do the squid start to run?" Wynn took a turn at the wheel and watched the depth finder closely. It may be early to tell, but it could be another generation with shrimp in their veins.

17

Cockspur Island Lighthouse

Situated at Fort Pulaski's easternmost point is a little brick lighthouse that weathered the storms of the Atlantic and of the Civil War.

17

Cockspur Island Lighthouse

The third Sunday in February I was out near the Cockspur Island Lighthouse when I saw a waving girl. But it was not Florence Martus greeting an arriving ship.

It was Fort Pulaski ranger Amber DeBardelaben, up to her knees in marsh mud. She was waving both arms to steady herself from falling over backward and taking a seat with the fiddlers. She was rescued by her Park Service comrades Katie Purcell and Candice Wyatt.

DeBardelaben was a little embarrassed because she had been warning us about the mud and the sharp oyster shells as we hiked out the trail to the lighthouse. She wasn't the first to misstep; as she was steadied and tugged each leg up, a captured flip-flop and a sneaker came out of the mud too.

This year is the Park Service's 100th anniversary, and on the third Sunday of each month, Fort

Pulaski is offering a special Centennial program. With 125 other folks, I was on the inaugural Lighthouse Trail Hike in February; March 20 is a bicycle tour of the island.

The easy trail to the lighthouse is like the path Florence Martus would have taken when her brother was lighthouse keeper from 1881-1884. And our power trio of guides covered the natural, cultural, and historical facets of our trek.

As we walked along the dikes, DeBardelaben talked about how the slaves who built them were experts in rice cultivation and flood control. Their work reclaimed the land from the marsh and built Cockspur Island.

As we passed through the woods, Wyatt described the vegetation. Under the shady corridor of red cedar, we walked over a soft carpet of russet catkins. She told of how British cannonballs in the Revolutionary War bounced off the fibrous palmetto logs of Fort Moultrie and led to South Carolina's state nickname. She described how Native Americans used the leaves of the yaupon holly in ceremonial teas.

As we crossed the marsh, she pointed out the dried heads of sea oxeye daisies. She talked about the succulent glassworts, whose ashes were used in glass making, and whose tips turn cranberry red in the fall.

Purcell talked about the mysteries yet to be discovered on the stretch from the fort to the lighthouse. How no one knows the significance of a line of boulders in the middle of the marsh. She talked about the Savannah Gray bricks used to construct the lighthouse, how they were made at the Hermitage Plantation, and were known to "drink water like a goat."

When we got to the wooden crosswalk on the trail, everyone gasped at the first glimpse of the lighthouse. Serene and isolated, she stands, weathered but heroic on the fragile spit at Cockspur's eastern tip. The whoosh from the wake of a container ship swept against her shore.

She was built in 1848. Her base, constructed in the shape of a prow pointing into the waves, has helped her withstand the punishing seas. But time and tides have taken their toll. In 2008 the Georgia Trust for Historic Preservation placed the lighthouse on its list of ten "places in peril."

Concerned Tybee and Savannah residents formed the Friends of Cockspur Island Lighthouse to save her before she might topple. Through their intercession, Congressman Jack Kingston secured $1.5 million which was used in 2012 to deposit a breakwater of granite rocks which has stabilized the islet on which she sits.

Two years ago the Friends group, working with Tom Bliss, Director of the UGA Shellfish Research Lab on Skidaway Island, placed two tons of oyster shells around the lighthouse. They moved 800 plastic-mesh bags from truck to boat to island, and like a bucket brigade, positioned them at strategic points. Their goal is to reestablish the oyster beds as a natural buffer to control erosion.

At this time, by federal order, the lighthouse and the land around it, which is exposed at low tide, is closed to the public. Park Service personnel have these last few months been repairing the exterior brick stairs which are regularly submerged. They are using historically accurate natural cement which will set in the few hours between tides.

They have removed the deteriorated porthole, sash, and fan windows and the door and are re-milling replicas in the Park's maintenance shop. Soon they will begin repair of the brick stairs which wind up the lighthouse interior.

The Friends group needs to raise money next for specialized scaffolding that will be necessary for brick repointing and repainting of the outside surface. And for repair of the iron railing that surrounds the parapet.

Working with the Park Service, the Friends' goal is to bring back the sea oats and sand that once surrounded the lighthouse. And to get her safe and sound for visitors to come inside and climb her 46 feet once again.

She has a rich history and has served ancient and modern mariners well. She has withstood hurricanes that have washed 20 feet up her sides. Two lighthouse keepers lost their lives in service to her. Cannonballs arced over her during the bombardment of Fort Pulaski during the Civil War.

The last keeper left in 1912 after the lighthouse was decommissioned. It was he who planted the sprawling fig tree and the pecan trees that grow in the Fort's parade ground. The lonely beacon was neglected until the Coast Guard turned her over to the Park Service in 1959.

LIGHT AND PIER. Constructed of brick on an oyster-bed foundation, the Cockspur Light stands only 46 feet tall. (Courtesy of Fort Pulaski National Monument.)

The 1934 Lighthouse Service Bulletin noted that a pair of bald eagles nested in the lighthouse and were often perched on the parapet railing. Ten years ago Bernie and Beverly Goode kayaked to it and discovered a barn owl nest and two owlets at the top of the steps inside. The mother was perched in the daylight above and flew past them as they left, brushing their heads to say goodbye.

The Fort's website www.nps.gov/fopu has great photos of the lighthouse and its history. And their Facebook page FortPulaskiNPS is enlightening every day.

Last year Friends founder Harvey Ferrell convinced Sharon Collins, host of "Georgia Outdoors" on GPB, to visit. She fell in love with the little light and produced a breathtaking episode about it, titled simply "The Lighthouse."

The Cockspur Island Lighthouse is a good thing we've been given, a part of what is home. Whether seen from the top of the Fort or Tybee's north end, from the Lazaretto Creek bridge, from a shrimp boat or a dolphin cruise, she stirs something joyous, like a candle in the window.

You can help her survive and shine on. Tax-deductible donations may be made at:

cockspurislandlighthouse.com

18

Color of the Coast

Bright, big, and happy as Hell, an exhibit of paintings captures the spirit of people who work on the water. Snappers and shrimps and crabs, oh my!

18

Color of the Coast

At the Ships of the Sea Museum on MLK right now there is an exhibition that is right out of The Prince of Tides. It is a celebration of local folks with salt water in their blood.

The show is titled "Low Country Callings: Goin' with the Flow." It is a small group of big portraits by Isle of Hope artist Carol Miller. Miller has captured in nine bright paintings the spirit and energy of people who earn their livings on, and derive their joy from, these coastal waters.

I know some of them and have heard of others, and Miller puts you right in the boat with them. You are rowing quietly with Arthur Brannen toward Burnt Pot Island. You are in the bow with Nanny Roberts as he loosens his booming voice with a sip of Pabst Old Style beer.

You are landing a big red snapper in 80 feet of water with Captain Judy Helmey, pulling a crab trap in Shipyard Creek with Tim Goodwin, shrimping the Daufuskie Breakers with Captain J.B. Riffle and John-Boy Solomon. You are picking boiled crabs at Pin Point with Odessa Famble and Leola Williams, marine surveying giant ships at the Ocean Terminal with David Peterson. You are waiting to see a mystery man on the Moon River send his cast net flying.

These are people who know the tides, know the names of every little creek, know who built this dock or that bateau. They know one another now and whose grandfathers and mothers worked with one another. They are called to this way of life; it's not nine to five; it's forever.

In the portrait "The Snapper Shot" you can see the glee in the eyes of Captain Judy and customer Kate Fowler as they land a 28-pound red snapper. The look in the snapper's eyes isn't as joyous, but Judy says that he didn't have to worry. "It is a thrill to catch a fish that beautiful. For seven years now, we have caught and released every snapper we've caught. We expertly prick the swim bladder, and they happily swim away."

Judy has been running charters for fifty years like her father before her. She was underage to do it at first and was known as the "illegal captain" until she was old enough to take the Coast Guard captain's test. Like daughter, like father, she happily reported that her Dad has just been inducted into the American Prohibition Museum which opens next month in City Market.

Judy was amazed at the accuracy in Miller's painting. "I was almost life size. And she captured the detail in the custom-made silver reel, the wrinkles

in my shirt, the gunwales, the fishing belt and lure."
Miller is good at that.

In "The Matriarchs of Pin Point" she captures the
history, the dignity in the faces of Odessa Famble and Leola Williams as they pick crabs near the
old Varn's Oyster Canning Factory where they both
once worked. Odessa's father Sammy Wiggins
managed the factory until it closed in 1985 after
sixty years of operation.

Nowadays the two women get together twice a week to pick crabs and make deviled crabs for family and friends. They relax and talk about church and chihuahuas. Ms. Williams lives in Savannah and still works at Candler Hospital where for close to 38 years her maternal touch has comforted day-surgery patients.

Ms. Williams' son is Supreme Court Justice Clarence Thomas, Odessa's friend from childhood. As they sit and pick crabs with nimble fingers, the women sometimes listen to Judge Judy or Judge Mathis on TV, but Ms. Williams says that she doesn't think her son watches those shows.

Tim Goodwin is tied to Pin Point too. The painting "The Crab Whistler" shows him pulling a pot not far from his home on Shipyard Creek. "As a boy I would hear the sounds of the putt-putts passing our house at 4:00 in the morning. Men going crabbing in their cypress boats, gray mariners, John

Henry Haynes and Richard Wiggins. When I close my eyes, I can hear them now."

Goodwin started crabbing at age 13 himself in a boat built for him by his grandfather. Even during his 30 years teaching mathematics at Savannah State, he has crabbed when class was out. Today he is one of the two licensed Georgia crabbers who pull their pots bare-handed.

And he whistles while he works. Some free-form tunes inspired by the time of day. Some songs he has written, songs that have come to him in dreams. "Many people on Moon River tell me how soothing it is to hear my peaceful whistling across the quiet marsh before dawn." It's part of a coastal soundtrack, and Goodwin says that usually his last look before going to bed at night is at the lights on the old Varn's docks.

The portraits of Captain J.B. Riffle and his striker John-Boy Solomon aboard the shrimp boat Agnes Marie capture their love of the waters between Lazaretto Creek and Calibogue Sound. Riffle empties the bag of a net full of shrimp onto the deck in the painting "The Blessing from W.G." Miller so titled the painting to honor the memory of William Glenn Smith, the captain who took Riffle under his wing 45 years ago and gave him his start in shrimping.

"I was with W.G. in Shallotte, N.C. when he built the Agnes Marie. I know the wood in her ribs, her

planks, her hull. When it came time for W.G. to retire, he sold her to me if I promised that he could work on her when his health permitted. I did that, and he was at her wheel the day he passed away. His spirit still lives in this boat."

"Sortin' the Final Drag" shows John-Boy Solomon awash in orange plastic baskets, separating shrimp from crabs and whiting. His Tybee family goes back generations, and, while he has done plumbing and electrical work his whole life, his happiest times are on the water. He got his striker's license at the age of seven.

"I love how everything comes full circle. When my mother was in high school, she worked summers as a striker on one of W.G.'s earlier boats in Thunderbolt. And I helped salvage W.G.'s son's boat the Odyssey when she sank 30 years ago on Daufuskie."

David Peterson also knows a bit about shipwrecks. He has been both a potter and a marine surveyor his whole life. Miller's painting "A Meld of Water and Clay" shows him at the Ocean Terminal, his strong arm on coils of steel, the bulk carrier Teizan and the Talmadge Bridge in the background.

His steel-blue eyes gaze, like the Cosmos Mariner, at destinations unknown. But away from the docks, his hands form ceramic dories and peapods from his native New England. He teaches ceramics at the City's Department of Cultural Affairs, and his studio is full of ship's hulls, all made of clay.

"The construction of a boat is artistic; the steaming and shaping of timbers have always fascinated me.

A ship is the ultimate art piece." His latest works are of actual historical shipwrecks, in which rigging, hulls, and cargo rest like ghosts in epoxied sand.

A ghost of another sort is Tony, who has become something of Miller's mystery man. Three years ago she photographed him casting for shrimp from the fishing bridge over the Moon River, but she only caught his first name. He was there with his wife and daughter and said that they came all the time on his days off.

Miller's painting "Pin Point Sunrise" shows him with the lead line of his cast net clenched in his teeth. If you meet him, tell him that Miller has a print and a special oyster for him. And that it's a calling.

19

The Secret's in the Salt

Two South Carolina brothers are building
an oyster business through clean water
and hard work. Their office is the
May River and Calibogue Sound.

19

The Secret's in the Salt

On a chilly afternoon last month Austin Harter handed me an oyster that he had just pulled from a bed on the banks of Bryan Creek. He popped open its shell, rinsed it in the water next to the boat, and held it for me in his muddy glove. "It should taste clean and salty," he said.

Let me tell you, it tasted cosmically clean and salty. That May River oyster was an exercise in purity. It was the pearl standard of freshness and tasty joy.

This past year I have heard people singing the praises of the May River Oyster Company in Bluff-ton. After my cruise with them out to their oyster beds and aquaculture cages, I've joined the choir. These guys are committed.

Brothers Austin and Andrew Harter (28 and 24 years old) are partners in the company with their uncle Brad Young. They grew up in Orangeburg but spent every summer in Bluffton. "We spent all our time outdoors - fishing, crabbing, shrimping, playing on the May River sand bar."

Both brothers have a background in food service but three years ago decided to make their passion for the river into their livelihood. It's hard work with heavy lifting. They do it on purpose; they were not out of work or between jobs. They are something like the Blues Brothers; they're on a mission from God.

Oyster beds are the filtration system for estuaries. They clean the waters of silt and pollutants and provide rich habitat for fish and invertebrates. The more oyster beds, the healthier the ecosystem.

Austin and Andrew are committed to "sustainability." They say that word about every minute. As we motored out to their lease grounds in their Carolina Skiff, Austin said with courteous pride, "Welcome to our office." And, as he swept his arm over the acres of marsh grass on either side of us, "How do you like the carpet?"

The brothers' sense of stewardship shows in their commitment to "do it the hard way, which is doing it the right way." Their lease covers most of the shores of Calibogue Sound. They harvest from existing oyster beds and from cages of farmed oysters.

On the wild beds, they practice what they call "culling in place." They do not clear cut. They take only the mature larger oyster clusters. That thinning allows the younger, smaller oysters to spread and grow.

They encourage customers to return their shells. On my trip with them, they dumped several bags of shells at spots where they could become the foundation for future beds. Oyster spat are drawn to settle onto exiting beds and shells.

When we anchored at Bryan Creek at low tide, Austin and Andrew went ashore with bushel baskets to work the grand gray strand. It was quiet as could be, not another boat in sight. There was only the sound of Austin's geologist hammer and Andrew's nail puller chinking into the beds and loosening oysters. Our only company was a willet stepping lightly on the mud and snacking on tiny crabs.

Besides harvesting clusters from the natural oyster beds, the brothers are growing their own through aquaculture. And that is a population explosion with several benefits. It reduces the pressure to overharvest and produces the luscious singles that restaurants love. And the more oysters in the water column, the cleaner the whole ecosystem.

It's hard work. The oysters grow in wire-mesh cages that sit just off the bottom. As the oysters grow, so do the cages. The brothers add tiers of larger mesh and transfer the larger oysters to the upper floors. Comes a satisfying day, and those oysters in the cage penthouses are gathered to go to local chefs.

They have to tend the cages all year long, watching for predators - from oyster drills to boring sponges to stone crabs and anything that may foul the mesh. I saw their routine as they winched up the hundred-pound cages full of prime singles.

They examined the oysters, stirring them around by hand and listening for the sound that meant they were full and healthy. They held them up to the light, looking for a deep cup and nice fan to the shell.

Andrew explained, "Even when it's not harvesting season (October into May), it's still growing season. We learn more every month about where the sweet spots are, the best depths to sit the cages, why the oysters in one cage are growing faster than those in another. It is a thrill to see them grow from seed oysters to table size, and to know that they have that pure, unique May River flavor."

The brothers get their seed oysters (only 2 to 5 millimeters) from the Lady's Island Oyster Hatchery. Lady's Island has perfected an orchestrated oyster spawning, bringing together the right eggs with the right sperm. Those good genetics make for single oysters that thrive in Low Country waters.

It takes from 10 to 16 months for the seed oysters to grow to a perfect three-inches. They are moved from mesh bags to the cages as they grow, all the while filtering the phytoplankton and nutrients in the pollution-free May River.

An oyster's taste comes from where it is grown. The May River is pure estuarine – no freshwater input, no factories, no cities, no pollution. Just bracing Atlantic saltiness.

The boys sent me home with a half-bushel bag that I steamed the next day. A friend who usually automatically coats everything he eats with sauce could not believe how sweet they were all by their tender selves.

Chef Tony Seichrist at the Wyld Dock restaurant, perched on Country Club Creek in Bonna Bella (right at the manatee crossing), is another big fan. He uses the May River clusters exclusively for oyster roasts and serves the aquaculture singles with special touches.

"They have a nuanced flavor, delicate and briny at the same time. The Harter boys and the oysters never let me down. By proxy I get to be close to the product."

He roasts and tops them with a little bacon fat, thyme, lemon, garlic, and bread crumbs. And he serves them chilled, raw-bar style, with frozen toppers like cucumber ginger, Meyer lemon, and horseradish ice.

Austin and Andrew care about the river and care about the culture. "We feel like we are part of a natural cycle that we can sustain and share."

While I was out with them, clouds would sweep their slow shadows across the marsh. Ripples spread over the quiet waters like divine fingerprints. Austin opened one oyster after another, pointing out that they were the color of an overcast sky.

"Look at that," he said. "There's your silver lining."

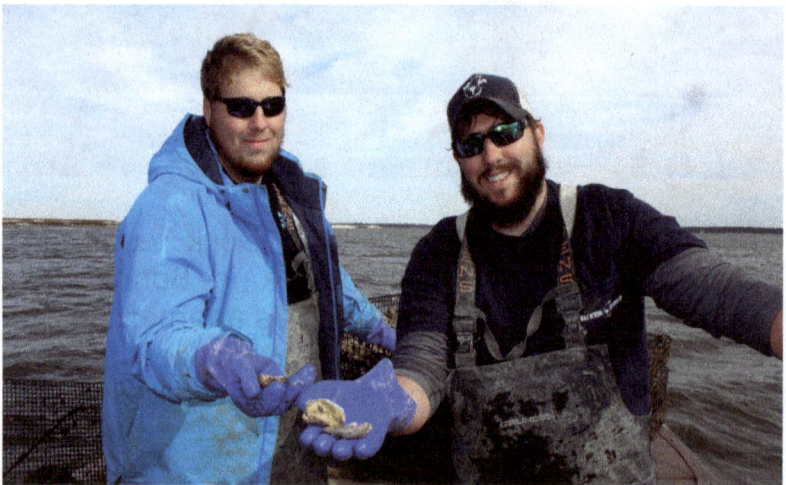

20

Shifting Baselines

A film about saving a way of life features families that have shrimped, oystered, and fished in Georgia waters for generations. The film makes your mouth water too.

20

Shifting Baselines

It was drizzly last Tuesday evening at the Tybee Post Theater, perfect weather for a good movie. It was the final night of summer's Gray's Reef film series, and the audience was gathered for a sneak peek.

We were viewing a test screening of "Shifting Baselines," a documentary of the Georgia coast and its fishing families. I was pumped because the last time I attended a test screening was for James Cameron's "Titanic," when I suggested that he insert the line "I'm the king of the world."

Local folks featured in the movie, legendary along the Georgia coast, were in the audience. Producer Cathy Sakas and director Mehmet Caglayan were there to take our every bit of feedback, to guide editing of the final cut for its premier at February's Gray's Reef Film Festival.

Before the show, photos from Gray's Reef cycled across the screen as Gary Strickland played the antique Steinway. His own song "Raining in Savannah" struck just the right chords.

The marine sanctuary lies just 19 miles east of Sapelo Island, and the serene reef scenes flowed with the music. Starfish cradled in the cups of basket sponges. Sea turtles gliding across the sand. Spadefish schooling like herds of zebra. Tiny silver minnows drifting like sequins in the tentacles of ghostly jellyfish. Spiny lobster, butterflyfish, vermilion snapper, all quiet among the waving sea whips.

The film opens and whets your appetite right off with a seafood dinner prepared by chefs Matt Roher of the Landings Club and Matthew Raiford of Brunswick's Farmer and Larder. You could smell the brine, the seasoning, as they worked with the wild Georgia shrimp, Sapelo clams, soft-shelled crab, and oysters.

Then the film moved to the families that have worked on the water for generations. Their faces and their voices all spoke of a heritage that defines the coast.

Oystering, shrimping, and fishing are in their blood. Many of their stories began with lessons taught by fathers and grandfathers. And carried the dignity of hard work that follows the tides and begins in the wee hours.

There was wisdom and laughter in the stories told by the Sonny Timmons family of Harris Neck; by Captain Judy Helmey of Wilmington Island; by Frank Cannarella Mathews of Savannah (whose leaping fish neon sign has shined on Congress Street since 1947); by Charlie Phillips of Townsend; by Howell Boone, Darwin and Wynn Gale of Darien.

But they all spoke of fisheries declining and of a way of life that may soon die because the country now imports over 90% of its seafood. The baselines may be shifting, but between the scientists, the chefs, and the fisherman a way forward can be found.

The fisheries can be managed to thwart "the tragedy of the commons." Like Captain Judy says, "We can make it the strategy of the commons. Sustainable seafood sustains the fishermen."

Boat to table is critical. The film dove into how successful fisherman, seafood markets, and restaurants are taking the layers of distribution out of the supply chain. Chef after chef said how they demand locally sourced, sustainable seafood. No orange roughy, no Chilean seabass, no imported shark.

I got a taste of that last month at First Presbyterian Church. Chef Kirk Blaine, owner of Castaways and Howlin' Hound restaurants, gave a cooking class "Summer's Bounty-Fresh Local Seafood" to benefit the transition program of the Good News Jail Ministry.

Blaine made the best cioppino this side of San Francisco. In addition to bay scallops and lobster, the garlicy tomato stew was full of local shrimp and clams. The sweet clams, courtesy of John Pelli's Savannah Clam Company, were harvested only a few miles away in Half Moon River off Wassaw Sound.

Blaine said, "We are all about fresh, local, sustainable. We have a 'You hook it, we cook it' program. You bring in your mahi, trout, redfish, crabs, cobia, and we create a four-course dinner for your party the next evening."

Captain Judy is an example of that same vision. Twenty years ago she could see that the red snapper fishery was heading toward collapse and that regulation was coming.

"We all took too much. Our charter business had been built on red snapper, but I started shifting the focus. I imposed my own limits on big fish, stricter than mandated. I started making more of everything we'd catch.

"To me it's a gift every day that I get to go out, and I convey that to my customers. I regale them with stories of my dad, him running liquor for Al Capone, him wrapping eel skins around his knees to prevent arthritis. I talk about the dolphins, the albatrosses, the Portuguese men-of-war, the black sea bass that change from female to male.

"Now that the red snapper fishery is closed, we release any that we catch. We use circle hooks so as not to wound them, and dip nets to land them gently.

"There's magic and meaning out there. I see it every time a customer first gets to the Gulf Stream. Something stirs in them. Deep down, something stirs."

21

Sea Turtles and Sand Fences

Sea turtles depend on the sand dunes for egg laying. The dunes are the first line of defense for every barrier island. Citizen science and citizen spirit keep it all from washing away.

21

Sea Turtles and Sand Fences

Saturday September 30 was an exciting day on Ty-bee Island. From the north end to the south, good things were happening. At 1:00, near the pavilion, to the cheers of hundreds of people, the Burton 4-H Center released Zoe, their five-year-old log-gerhead sea turtle.

And earlier, from 9:00 until noon on the north beach, some hard work was done that will benefit not only Zoe and her kin, but also all of her cheer-ing fans. Who knew that a sand-fencing project could be so exciting? With its own high-fives and cheering when the job was complete.

The City of Tybee's Beach Task Force had put out a call for volunteers for the dune-building project. "Come with post-hole diggers, work gloves, and a willing attitude." And 75 sand-angels answered the call.

They dug holes, sunk poles, strung fencing between them, and piled up marsh-grass wrack against them. And they did it like a well-oiled machine. Like they did it every weekend. What they left on the beach was better than it looked on the drawing board.

The fencing will build dunes that will protect the island from storm surges and wave action. The design was new and innovative, and it will be monitored

quarterly to see how effectively sand accretes and dune plants take hold. It's a herringbone-like arrangement with angled rows of fences to trap sand as it blows from offshore, onshore, or longshore.

Georgia DNR had to evaluate and approve the design as turtle-friendly, with the fences spaced and oriented so as not to thwart or stress sea turtles coming ashore to lay eggs.

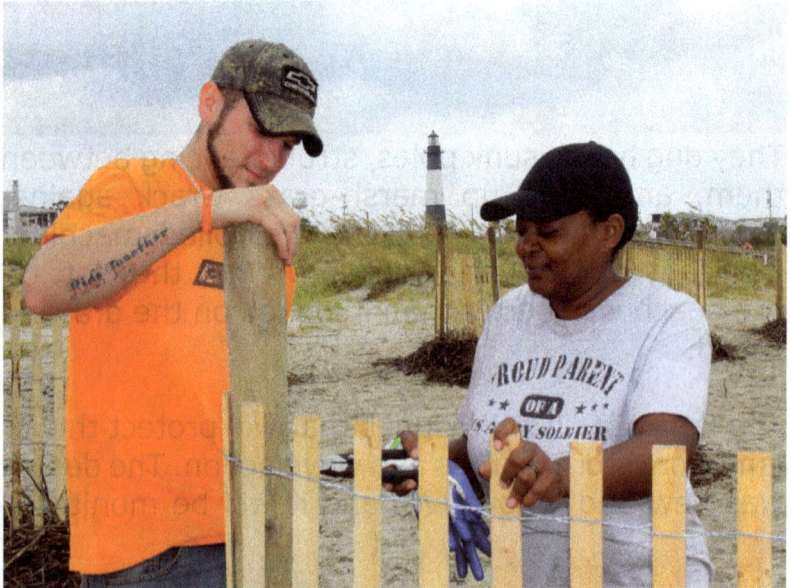

The project was a big job, covering about 100 yards by 50 feet. Folks dug 148 holes. Young and old, these were people who love Tybee and the ocean world.

Jessie, Duane, and Austin Miles came from Rincon. Jessie said, "We are all about helping. We came down a week ago to work in homes on Chatham Avenue that had flooded from Hurricane Irma. When we heard about this project, we knew that we had to be here."

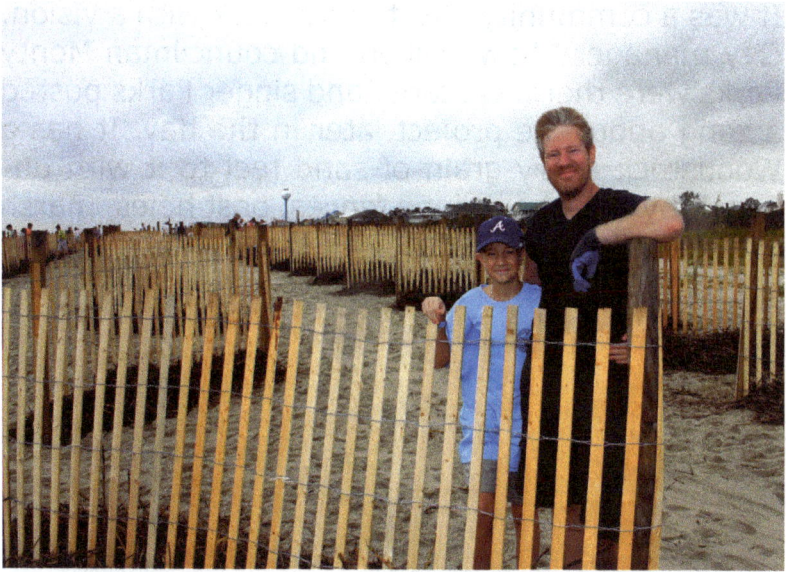

Gordon Grant-Tweedie and his son Logan were thrilled to be playing a part. "Logan's in Boy Scout Troop 1, and that's how we heard about this. He's very interested in marine life and ecology. Years from now, when dunes stand here, we can point them out with pride and say, 'I helped build that.'" Heard Elementary teacher Billie Cassidy was there with her husband. A week earlier she and her fellow first-grade teachers had walked the same beach with a hundred students. "We teach the kids to think globally and act locally. They got good instruction here about the impact of litter. It's amazing what a bunch of six-year-olds with grabbers can do."

Their lesson had come from Tim Arnold of Tybee Clean Beach Volunteers. The logo on their Facebook page, Fight Dirty Tybee, is a loggerhead with red boxing gloves. For the dune-fencing project, his group supervised 15 UGA students who picked litter out of the wrack before it was placed at the feet of the fences.

It was a community effort, hard work with a vision. City manager Shawn Gillen and councilman Monty Parks were there. Guitarist and singer Parks posted a song about the project later in the day. It has a Woodstock every-grain-of-sand feel to it with unusual rhymes about dune fences, post holes, marsh wrack, and loggerheads.

If Zoe turns out to be a girl, she'll come back to Tybee in 25 years to lay her eggs. The Parks' song might be a standard by then, and the dunes she climbs may have been started on the day of her release.

Right now she's a healthy specimen, the size of an 8-to-10-year-old naturally-occurring loggerhead. That's because of the TLC that she has received during her five years at the Center, where she has been a star to 35,000 to 40,000 kids.

Director Paul Coote explained that visiting students and campers typically do some beach seining, and that Zoe always got to eat some of the catch - fresh shrimp, crabs, and jellyfish. In addition she ate a DNR-prescribed diet, rich in vitamins and minerals.

Before her release, she was outfitted with a transmitter that allows researchers to track her. She was raised in a 1500-gallon tank, but she seems to be enjoying the wide-open spaces now.

Her location will soon be continuously available on a satellite-tracking website, but for now you can see her travels on the Burton 4-H Center Facebook page. She first swam pretty far offshore, then back to Little Tybee and Wassaw Sound. Then offshore again and back to Ossabaw Sound. As I write here on Oct. 5, yesterday she was poking around the Little Ogeechee River and this morning around Raccoon Key.

While he was toting bundles of fencing at the north end, Kevin Smith of Oatland Island was humming "Don't fence me in." "This is great. All these people. It's like an Amish barn raising, many hands making light work. Good for the environment; good for the dunes; good for the soul."

22

The Tybee Cemetery

The serene Tybee Cemetery lies in the middle of Memorial Park. Mysteries surround many of those who rest there, mariners and settlers of multiple nationalities.

22

The Tybee Cemetery

Wearing medals that he had just bought for his grandson at the Forever Tybee yard sale in Memorial Park October 10, Alan Roach walked to the Tybee Cemetery just steps away.

"I guess that I am about as forever Tybee as you can get. My grandson is the sixth generation. My great-grandfather was an Ohio farmer who came as a reluctant tourist with General Sherman. After the war, he came back."

"When I was a kid, we played baseball at the diamond right over there and chased home runs into this little cemetery. It's full of good memories for me. But a lot of its own history is a mystery."

It seems that the town's cemetery grew around the family plot of the Wortham family. In the 1870's Englishman George Wortham settled on Tybee and farmed a large parcel of land. He looked after the town's waterworks, managed the Ocean House hotel, and ran a horse-and-buggy service from the landing at Lazaretto Creek to the south end of the island. His wife was the town's first postmistress and operated the post office out of the old Martello Tower.

The oldest marked grave belongs to William H. Clark, who passed away in 1876 at age twenty. He was an assistant lighthouse keeper.

A beautiful marble headstone marks the grave of 17-year-old German sailor, H. Max G. Eggert, who

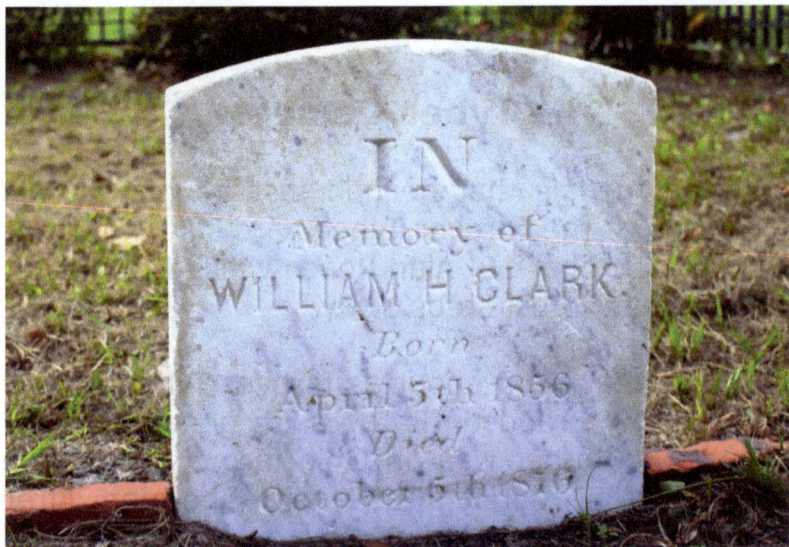

fell overboard while his ship was anchored in the Savannah River in 1879. The headstone, commissioned by his mother and shipped from Germany, stands as a timeless tribute to her son. Its closing words – "Here gently rest his ashes."

Scotsman Alexander McKenzie's grave lies between graceful spider lilies. He was a famously gregarious character. In 1872, after a newborn baby wrapped in a shawl was found in Savannah and entrusted for a few days to a caring widow, McKenzie carried the child home to his wife as a surprise. The baby was christened on Tybee and named Eliza Jane, raised by the McKenzies, and forever known as the "little waif."

Between 2003 and 2005 the Tybee Beautification Committee did historical research about the 14 people named on existing markers and 5 others named in a 1922 city inventory. With ground-penetrating radar they determined a total of 36 burial sites.

They unraveled the questions behind some markers, like the one assumed to be for three Rotureau brothers who were "washed ashore" in 1876. Interviews with descendants revealed that the initials on the stone were for a husband, wife, and child who died at later dates, none from shipwreck. Presumably the inscription came as an error on a replacement marker or as a poetic reference to "crossing the bar" since the father had been a ship captain.

The latest burial in the cemetery is William A. Jennings in 1952. He was the director of the Chamber of Commerce and had been the driving force in dedicating Memorial Park itself in 1947 as a tribute to Tybee men who died in WWII. A descendant remembered him as the man who discovered the tunnel from the Pirates House to the Savannah River.

On every recent visit to the cemetery I have met locals who cherish it. City arborist Brent Levy was there checking on the large multi-trunk live oak that shades the five Wortham graves. He said that he is looking forward to the camellias flowering next month.

Tybee Beautification members Bernie and Beverly Goode had bicycled over to meet Allan and Sara Jones to look at the most recent plaque that graces the large memorial wall. It commemorates John Davant, ancestor of Tybee resident Doug Webb. Poor Davant, one of Oglethorpe's settlers, died in 1733 after only one month on the island.

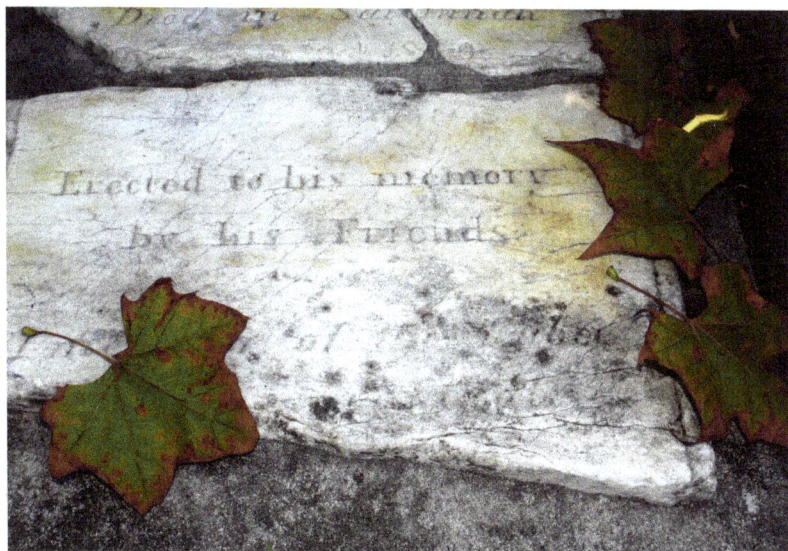

Tybee mayor Jason Buelterman came jogging by with his daughter Anna and stopped to talk and look at the newly-placed plaque for Danny Williams. Williams died in a tugboat accident off Tybee last year.

Shirley Sessions comes often with her sister Sandy McCloud to place flowers and to rest on the bench dedicated to their mother Eloise Carroll and lifelong friend Don Norton. "This is such a peaceful place. I never tire of sitting here and looking at the three cherubs holding hands and seeming to dance on a cloud of asparagus ferns."

The first ashes scattered in the cemetery after its refurbishment and dedication in 2005 were those of Anne Monaghan. Her plaque was also first. Written by her husband, it reads "I love you Honey." His own now stands next to hers and reads "Together Again."

The plaque for Danny Williams, composed by his mother Arden, reads "Loving Son, Loyal Friend,

Dedicated Mariner." On October 28 family and friends will gather at the cemetery for a memorial service.

"He came to be a mariner in a serendipitous way. He was a trained chef and worked at numerous restaurants. But he met a tugboat captain at the Vidalia Onion Festival and six weeks later was on the boats, cooking and working as an able-bodied seaman. Seven years where he had found his destiny."

"He felt part of a maritime brotherhood. We are from Grantville, far inland, but on these salt waters, of Tybee and Savannah, he found a second home."

23

Pink Eye Candy

Roseate Spoonbills are splashes of pink in Georgia marsh landscapes. Birdwatching punsters may chide, "You Audubon there."

23

Pink Eye Candy

Years ago my wife and I were cruising at dusk, enjoying the evening glow over the marsh at Horse Pen Hammock. Suddenly dramatic dabs of pastel in the top of a weathered tree stopped us in our tracks.

Two large birds rested there like pink cotton candy, like pink fleecy clouds, like serenity in feathers. They were Roseate Spoonbills, rare birds we were lucky to see. We looked for them afterwards, but that single sweet day was our only glimpse.

January 20 I was down in Richmond Hill for the annual symposium hosted by the Coastal WildScapes organization. They sponsored a photo contest this year to focus on the beauty of Georgia's beaches and barrier islands. A slideshow of those photographs cycled before the lectures.

Beautiful photos one after another of boneyard beaches, waterspouts, blue crabs, jellyballs, herons, and egrets. Then déjà vu! Splash, and splash again, two of the best photos of roseate spoonbills that I have ever seen.

They were taken by Elma Andrews of Saint Simons Island who has loved the birds since first seeing them in the Florida Keys in the 1980's. These photos were closer to home: a treetop pair like my wife and I saw, and a flock wading next to the causeway in the "marshes of Glynn."

"They are becoming more common here these last several years. I am fascinated by the soft pink feathers with streaks like lipstick on their shoulders. And the pollen yellow around their eyes and under their throats."

"Their faces actually look prehistoric, and the ruby irises of their bright eyes look like deep-space images of ring nebulae. I most like their bills that are shaped like the wooden spoons my grandmother used."

"They use their bills to sift through marsh bottom, feeling for minnows, shrimp, crabs, and crayfish. When they are courting, they present sticks to each other and cross and clasp their bills together; that gives an added meaning to the romantic term 'spooning.'"

I soon realized that this is not only the Chinese year of the dog, but also the year of the spoonbill, at least in my world. Staring out at you from the poster for Coastal WildScapes' next event is James Audubon's 1836 engraving of the roseate spoonbill.

That event is "Starlight and Spartina – An Evening under the Oaks" this Saturday at the Musgrove Plantation on St. Simons Island. The spoonbill on the poster is captured in all his pink glory, the water below his bill rippling from his last dip and his bright eye seeming to extend an invitation.

As Christopher Walken once said, "I need more spoonbill." At the event, throw pillows, napkins, and reusable utensil sleeves from Wendy Barnes Design will make their debut, with elegant silhouettes of spoonbills and sea oats.

"The spoonbill is my favorite bird, and I love how sea oats stabilize sand dunes." Both Barnes and Coastal WildScapes received One Hundred Miles 100 awards this year for their work to protect and preserve the Georgia coast.

The Starlight and Spartina evening features a tour of Musgrove Plantation's gardens and historic buildings, following in the footsteps of guests like President Jimmy Carter and King Hussein of Jordan. There is a falconry demonstration by Brunswick's On the Fly Outfitters. There is music by Tonic Blue, heavy hors d'oeuvres, and auction items focused on experiences in nature.

Starlight and Spartina

AN EVENING UNDER THE OAKS

Saturday, March 3rd, 2018
Musgrove Plantation, Saint Simons Island

www.coastalwildscapes.org

Shirts with the poster image will be available, so that will take care of my spring wardrobe. I may catch the attention of the spoonbills that are now nesting at the St. Augustine Alligator Farm Zoological Park. Photographer Andrews says that the park has the best rookery around.

"They have acres of wetlands. It is fenced in and, since it's full of alligators, bird predators like raccoons don't dare to venture in. The egrets, herons, and spoonbills all nest in peace in the tree tops."

Andrews' spoonbill photos and others from the contest will be on display from April 13 to May 14 at the Old Jail Art Center in Darien.

Audubon noted the graceful steps of the spoonbill and compared its color to the scarlet ibis and the American flamingo. He was fascinated by its unique bill and feeding behavior.

Florida children's author and poet B. J. Lee captures that and more in her limerick:

Her bill is a long slotted spoon.
She dips it down in the lagoon.
With hoovering swishes
she captures small fishes
in the pink on a June afternoon.

24

Sift and Seine

Educators at the Tybee Island Marine Science Center have groups get wet and sandy as they discover the amazing and elusive creatures at the Edge of the Sea.

24

Sift and Seine

A good teacher can have an influence over a lifetime of tidal cycles. Especially a good science teacher.

As a student at BC in the 1960's, I was lucky to have one like that. Our science teacher Ashton Varnedoe put kinetic energy into every lesson. My classmates still crack up recalling his herky-jerky, full-body demonstrations of molecular attraction – alternating between the roles of Mickey Molecule and Minnie Molecule.

In Biology class Mr. Varnedoe introduced us to the incredible nature writer Rachel Carson. Week after week we heard about her book "Silent Spring," DDT, and the thinning shells of eagle's eggs. On the first day of class, each student got a paperback of one of her books to do a report on: "Under the Sea Wind," "The Sea Around Us," or "The Edge of the Sea."

I was one of the third who got "The Edge of the Sea." Like Lt. Dan's "magic legs" in "Forrest Gump," the pages in that book were magic glasses, allowing us to see things previously unseen or overlooked. Plants and animals in the web of life, on rocky shores, in tide pools, on jetties and docks, and in the waves and sand of the Georgia shore.

Like fortunate students, locals and visitors to Savannah alike are lucky to have the Tybee Island Marine Science Center as a great resource, right here at the water's edge. The aquariums are full of local marine life, and the teaching staff are right out of Mr. Varnedoe's mold.

They offer daily beach walks, turtle talks, marsh treks, and what I went on last week – the hands-on "Sift and Seine" beach activity. Program Director Beth Palmer first had us digging into the wet sand, sifting it, and washing what was caught on the screens into a bucket of water.

Then she explained what we caught. There were lots of tiny, twitching, translucent amphipods, that look like little shrimp. They live among the sand grains, eating bacteria and plant debris, and are eaten themselves by small fish and even sea horses.

There were many small coquina clams that inhabit the surf zone, feeding on plankton that they siphon from the water as waves break, then quickly burrowing into the sand as the waves recede so as to hide from birds who want to eat them. Palmer said that, because the two sides of coquina shells often stay together when they die, beachcombers call them butterfly wings.

Palmer asked what might explain the beveled holes that appeared to have been drilled into the numerous cockle shells that we collected. Nine-year-old Owen Pursley knew the answer, "Either a dog whelk or a moon snail. With its radula." Palmer explained that the moon snails found all over our beaches have mouth parts like rasps that allow them to drill holes into the bivalves that they love to eat.

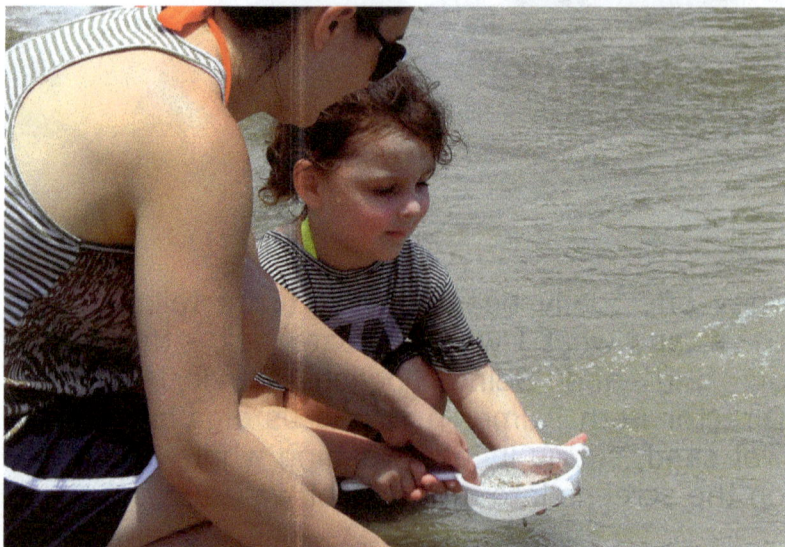

Palmer handled a number of glistening jingle shells and explained that they take their name from how they sound jingling in your hand. They are thin-walled and delicate with a beautiful pearlescence. Crushing the shells to a powder, she explained that the particles are called mermaid's makeup and are used in cosmetics. Three-year-old Elsa Boelhave and I were eager to spread some on our cheeks.

Next Palmer led our group in using a short seine net to dip under and sweep through the waves. We caught schools of juvenile whiting and pompano. Palmer said that they also routinely catch silversides, shrimp, and mullet, but that you never know when something unusual might show up.

"Last week a boy said that he hoped to catch a sea spider like he had seen on the TV show 'The Octonauts.' And we caught one, the first one that I have ever seen! Sometimes we catch jellyfish, speckled crabs, whelk egg cases, or the leathery egg-collars of moon snails."

Our Sift-and-Seine group was quite cosmopolitan: the Boelhave family (Jody, Andrea, Milo, and Elsa)

from Kentucky; father and son Steve and Owen Pursley from West Virginia; Girl Scout curriculum expert Michelle Schmidt from Kansas along with Scout Ambassadors Gabs Fuentes, Anna Schmidt, and Sadie Lucier.

Schmidt and the girls, high-school seniors, also took the Beach Walk tour, led by Marine Science Educator Alli Williford, and loved it. They saw dolphins, burrowing sand dollars, and sea turtle nests, and learned about dune structure and sea oats.

Schmidt exclaimed, "You are all so lucky to live by the edge of the sea, so close to the rhythm of nature." That sounded just like something Mr. Varnedoe would say.

25

Lost at Sea

Two months before the end of WWI 130 Georgia farmboys-turned-soldiers went down with the ship in a storm on a Scottish shore. A memorial to them stands at Fort Screven where they trained.

25

Lost at Sea

Like a message in a bottle, the story of a WWI shipwreck washed into the life of John Calvert. It's a tragedy that started almost in his front yard at Fort Screven on Tybee Island a century ago.

On September 19, 1918, in the waning days of the Great War, 580 new recruits under the command of Lt. Sam Levy boarded a train at Fort Screven bound for New York. From there they would sail to Britain to join the war on the battlefields of France.

Aboard the British troopship HMS Otranto, the flagship of a convoy of 13 ships, they departed New York on September 25. Hurricane season. U-boat season.

The Atlantic crossing was storm-tossed. Soldiers were seasick days on end. The Spanish flu, which was raging worldwide, took the lives of some.

On the morning of October 6, off the Scottish island of Islay, tragedy struck. In 60-foot seas and a Force 11 gale, a sister ship, the HMS Kashmir collided with the Otranto, tearing a massive hole in her hull. She was dead in the water.

Under wartime orders the crippled Kashmir continued on her way. But defying those orders, Lt. Francis Craven brought his escort destroyer HMS Mounsey alongside the much-larger Otranto four times to attempt a rescue. Man after man jumped from the Otranto to the decks of the Mounsey.

Many were swept away; many were crushed between the ships. But by the heroism of the Mounsey crew 590 men were saved, over 300 of them Americans. Every Ft. Screven soldier who survived owed his life to Lt. Craven's bravery. His ship the Mounsey was so damaged that it never again saw action.

Within three hours the Otranto crashed onto Islay's rocky shore. Of the men still aboard, less than 20 survived the raging surf and grinding wreckage. Those who did were pulled to safety by islanders, holding on to shepherds' crooks, the length of life and death.

With solemn reverence, islanders buried almost 400 casualties from the Otranto. Women sewed a large US flag for the funeral. They sang the US and British national anthems, and a bagpiper played "Flowers of the North."

The hand-sewn flag now rests in the Smithsonian, but it returned to Islay this spring. Under the 80-foot stone tower erected by the Red Cross after the war, Britain's Princess Anne led a centennial commemoration.

GRAVES OF "OTRANTO" MEN AT KILCHOMAN, ISLAY.   PHOTO CAMERON, BOWMORE.

The sinking of the Otranto was the single greatest loss of life in troop transport during the war. 470 US and British servicemen died. 130 of those were Georgia boys, many working on their farms just months earlier. Eleven were from Chatham County.

The message in a bottle that came to John Calvert, of Tybee's American Legion, was a book "Many Were Held by the Sea" that told the Otranto story. In it are listed those who were lost.

From Savannah they were:
Andrew John Andrews
William W. Carter
Thomas L. Davis
Roy Dearman
Henry E. Gaudry
Gordon S. Hickman
John Alexander Hutton, Jr.
George W. Lowden, Jr.
Joseph H. Oppenheim
Ralph Scott Ray
William Eugene Warth

SAM LEVY [ON RIGHT] 1917

Fortunate survivors are listed too. Local names like Delaney, Hall, Horton, Ingram, Leonard, Miller, Mitchell, Rauber, and von Waldner.

Lt. Levy, who had commanded those doughboys, held reunions for survivors until his own passing in 1968. At those gatherings he offered prayers for those who had been lost.

This Saturday, September 15, Lt. Levy's grandson Chuck Freedman and other Otranto descendants return to Tybee. They come to unveil a historic marker in front of the Museum at Battery Garland, in the shadow of the lighthouse, near grounds where their ancestors would have drilled.

Two special British and American flags will be raised. They were flown underwater, carried by divers last month, draped over the guns of the Otranto.

The program will unfold with songs by Island Harmony and bagpipes. Tybee's mayor and other officials will speak. Additionally a storyboard telling the comprehensive history of the Otranto will be unveiled.

Artifacts recovered from the Otranto will be displayed. Visitors are invited for lunch at the American Legion and for tours of the nearby enlisted men's barracks.

At the Post Theater the new BBC documentary "Islay: For Those in Peril" will be shown. A young doughboy will read from the journals of Otranto survivor Joseph Hewell, as threads of bravery and kindness weave together the fates of Georgia boys cast on a Scottish shore.

26

Drowning in Zinnias

The zinnia is Tybee's official flower. They thrive in the heat like all Tybee residents, especially our own Miss Rumphius.

Drowning in Zinnias

When Tybee Garden Club member Jan Will closes her eyes, she dreams of zinnias. Miles and miles of zinnias. Patches along every fence, waving in patches against the dunes, patches shimmering around the water towers. Zinnias everywhere you look.

Will would like the zinnia to become Tybee's official city flower. I learned how passionate she was about them when I slowed to compliment her on the bright hundred that she was watering behind her picket fence on Campbell Avenue. She was nearly concealed behind the shoulder-high bursts of color.

She explained that she had become a champion of the zinnia after reading the children's book "Miss Rumphius" by Barbara Cooney. Will is an artist, educator, and school psychologist who retired to Ty-bee a few years ago. An old friend who visited to help with decorating sent her the book afterward with the note that "this is your life story."

After I read it, Will explained the parallels. I am amazed that a children's book, a lovely fiction, can inspire a retiree to follow that fiction to create something beautiful. But Robert Fulghum said, "all I really need to know I learned in kindergarten." So the lessons of "Miss Rumphius" are not confined to youth.

The book is about a little girl named Alice who gets guidance for life from her grandfather. She envisioned that, when she grew up, she would travel to faraway places and finally come home to live by the sea. He told her that there was a most import-ant third thing to do. "You must do something to make the world more beautiful."

Will said she was struck by how the little story resonated. Alice adventured in faraway places; Will has sailed the Amazon, trekked through Tibet, shivered in Antarctica and Iceland. Alice worked in a library; Will was a teacher. Alice fell off a camel; Will fell off an elephant. Alice painted the blue sky in her grandfather's landscapes; Will has painted the sky above Giverny.

In the book Alice retires to an island town with beautiful sunrises and sparkling water. She plants a small patch of lupines and finds them spread far and wide by the wind. So she sows lupine seeds everywhere across her island to "make the world more beautiful."

That story inspired Will. Her little pack of zinnia seeds thrived and then sprouted up everywhere downwind from her garden. So zinnias are her contribution, her opportunity, to make Tybee even more beautiful.

She is not alone. I posted on Nextdoor Tybee, and
zinnia testimonials and photos poured in. For Lynn
Schweitzer on Jones Avenue they grow all summer

and reseed into October. Deb Baber's bed along TS Chu Terrace fascinates tourists. Ruth MacKay's 5th Avenue yard is full of volunteers that blew from her flower boxes.

Kathryn Propst's plot in Tybee's Community Garden overflows with zinnias all summer. "I only bought seed once; they re-seed like crazy. They like hot, dry weather and stay bright when everything else withers."

Shirley Sessions reflected, "My grandmother would prepare the soil, scatter seeds by hand, and they bloomed forever, attracting hummingbirds and butterflies. The more she shared with neighbors, the more they grew."

Gardener Lisa D. Watson of Plan It Green Design loves zinnias because they are old-fashioned and surrounded her granny's home. She plants milkweed with them for monarch butterfly larvae and fennel for swallowtail larvae.

Chuck Powell said, "I grow zinnias every summer on 18th Street in memory of my mother, Frances Powell. She and I planted them together in the 1950's in Edgemere on 54th and Live Oak Streets."

Debbie Cameron has grown zinnias for 20 years. "They are so colorful and bright; they make me feel happy! I've been blessed to be able to share bouquets of zinnias with neighbors, coworkers, family, friends, and complete strangers. I think having this opportunity to bless others with cheerful zinnias is why I love them so much."

Allen Lewis and Jane Bridges grow zinnias every year on their third-floor porch where it is a real

floral stress test. "We face Chimney Creek; the western exposure subjects them to baking sun all afternoon, yet they thrive, re-seed, and send up volunteers. The more you cut them, the more they grow."

"Zinnias are very much like people on Tybee. They are generous; the more you get, the more they give; they are beautiful in many different ways."

27

Seagulls at Sunrise

One of many snowbirds who come south in the winter, Indiana's Joe Lawson has a morning ritual that popcorn-loving seagulls eat up.

Seagulls at Sunrise

Joe Lawson and his wife Meri travel every winter from Indiana to Tybee Island and stay for three months at Rivers End Campground. And every morning, before dawn's early light, Joe takes a little walk for a front-row seat to the greatest show on earth. The admission is free, and so is the popcorn.

He gets up well before sunrise and walks up Polk Street to the beach, where he walks north, then east. "I like to go past the point there, where depending on what the tide is doing, you can see a pretty clear place where the river meets the ocean." He walks toward the lighthouse and sits down near the long rock jetty on the North Beach.

He travels light, toting only a camp chair, an old Stanley thermos full of black coffee, and a bag of popcorn, no butter, no salt. The chair and the coffee are for Joe; the popcorn is for the seagulls.

"I love to watch the sunrise; I love to be in the presence of the ocean. I'm a spiritual person. It's pitch dark when I get there; the stars are shining like diamonds. Then the sky begins to get a tiny bit lighter and lighter; I love to watch the sky change colors. Then finally there is the moment when the sun peaks up over the water. It is a very powerful time of the day for me."

It also turns out to be a rewarding time of the day for the flock of ring-billed gulls that gather around

Joe every morning. "I call them my meditation buddies. I have worked out a lot of problems, setting on the beach, waiting for the sun to come up."

After sunrise, Joe feeds the seagulls, who have waited with him. "They know the routine." He showed me some cellphone photos. Some were of gulls perched on his head. Several were of one gull,

perched on his fingers and eating popcorn from his hand. "They've got the softest little feet with tiny claws on the ends. He wraps his feet around my fingers and eats out of the palm of my hand."

That particular gull remembers Joe from year to year. He is always the first to get close and comfortable. Besides his behavior Joe can identify him

from a peculiar marking on the side of his ring-bill. "You have to be close to see it. It's like somebody with a quivering hand drew it with a magic marker."

It's an observation an artist would make. Joe's wife Meri has painted all her life, and she got him started painting twenty years ago after he retired from GM as a tool and die maker. "I enjoy working with my hands."

He takes lessons during the year back home in Indiana; he does still lifes of "manly" subjects: cowboy boots and revolvers; baseball bats, balls, and gloves; block planes with wood shavings. "I think there is beauty in the color and curls of those shavings."

Here on Tybee he studies with Denise Vernon. He showed me a painting called "Reflection." It's an old man fishing from a pier and remembering when he sat on the same pier as a boy. He showed me another of an egret at the Bacon Park golf course.

Another painting was from a photo, taken by an early morning beachcomber, of Joe and the gulls, fiery light in the sky and on the water. He's not satisfied with it. "It was a spectacular sunrise, but

I wasn't able to capture the aura of being there." I think though that he came close, with the sun's rays shining through the gull's outermost feathers. "I can mix beautiful colors on my palette, but they don't hold a candle to the sky colors that God creates. Sometimes there are colors on the bottoms of the clouds that flash for only an instant. Not only does God do spectacular work, but He works quick."

Joe gets there an hour before sunrise. "The wind and the waves make a quiet, soothing white noise." The gulls come one at a time. They squawk for a while but then sit quietly, waiting patiently with him.

Popcorn is served only after sunrise. "They know the rule." Given the serenity, given the grace, given the point of light that stirs over the waters, it's clearly a golden rule.

28

The People's Parade

Tybee loves its parades. John Mellencamp's "I was born in a small town" could have been written about Tybee's January MLK parade. Usually cold; always cool.

The People's Parade

Tybee's John Mellencamp used to sing "I was born in a small town." On January 12 the TybeeMLK Parade and Human Rights Forum flowed like a lyric from that song. It was the best of small-town America, the best of Martin Luther King's dream.

Sometimes an event is billed as a celebration, but it doesn't quite come off. This one did. This one was fun. The weather was balmy, and spirits were fresh as a Tybee breeze.

The American Legion Post 154 honor guard's flags waved just right. The music was the perfect blend. The Brazilian percussion of Samba Savannah set the hips of parade watchers swaying. The Jimmy Buffett soundtrack that wafted from the Crab Shack float continued the contentment. Johnson High School's marching band, drum majors, and majorettes got viewers high-stepping in place.

Small-town closeness was evident in the walkers and riders: Tybee mayor Jason Buelterman, US Congressman Buddy Carter, Sheriff John Wilcher, former state senator Regina Thomas, former Tybee mayor Walter Parker. Grand marshal school superintendent Ann Levett was beaming.

In a cool rhyming stroke, she was followed by a string of cars belonging to the Savannah Corvette Club. (Levett, corvette, I get it.) Tybee council members walked and rode bicycles. There were people walking dogs; there were dogs walking cats; there were walking baby teeth.

There were beauty queens: Miss Savannah State University Aliyah Davis and Miss Black Georgia US Ambassador Ashleigh Montford. There were members of the Masjid Jihad mosque, Mickve Israel synagogue, All Saints Episcopal Church, St. Michael's Catholic Church, the Tybee Bar Church. There were Tybee Island Maritime Academy students and principal Pat Rossiter. Tybee Tots and Clemson fans walked. The Tybean Art and Coffee Bar, WRHQ

Quality Rock, Fannies on the Beach, and Yardman Lawn Care all cruised.

There was candy enough that kids hand-delivered it to parade watchers. One young man in blue plaid walked the route inviting people to write or draw in his notebook. A sweet little girl drew her charm bracelet.

That's kind of what the parade and forum were. A charm bracelet, each charm with its own importance. Every walker, every float, every corvette a link in the chain.

The forum at the YMCA, against a wall of paintings by children of Loop It Up Savannah, brought youth into focus. Students Salah Washington and Kate Bossler did the welcomes.

Salah told a story he learned from his imam. To buy some free time from his energetic son, a father gave him an educational jigsaw puzzle. It was a 195-country world map that he hoped would occu-

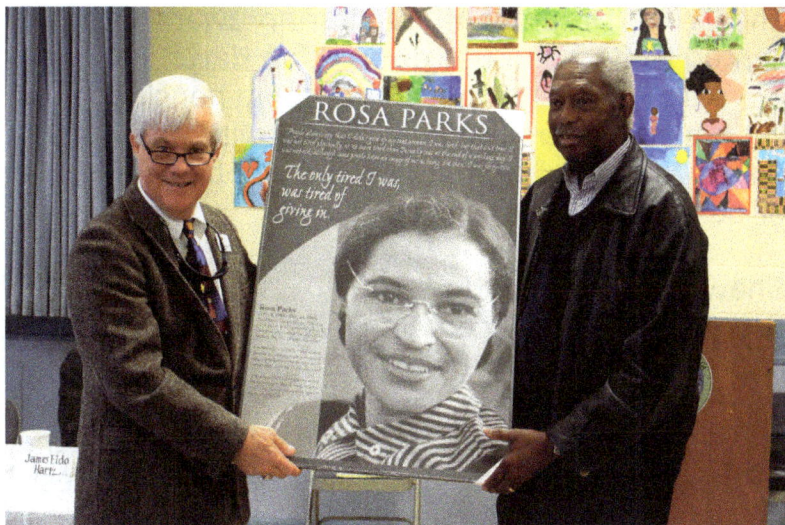

py junior all day, but his son returned in minutes, the puzzle done. He had found that on the reverse side was the figure of a man and putting those pieces together was easy. "I put the man together, and the world came together."

Kate tied Dr. King's message to Jewish belief that all men are equal in God's eyes. When Kim Polote then sang "The Impossible Dream," every phrase seemed richer. "The world will be better for this."

Islands High School juniors Camilla Burg and Anna Nguyen read their winning essays on Dr. King's "Letter from Birmingham Jail." Moving forward, Camilla is learning Korean, and Anna wants to work with Doctors without Borders.

The NAACP's Richard Shinhoster presented a portrait of Rosa Parks to principal Rossiter who said, "Our kids are very familiar with her; we honor her bravery as she sought to right the unrightable wrong; we tell them they have to find their own place on the bus of life."

The Tybee Dreamer Humanitarian award was presented to Carbo House owner Eldo Hartz. For twenty years his inn has been affordable housing for local police officers, seniors, hospitality and nursing home workers, "people who are the heart and soul of our community."

Shawn Bulloch, Bartlett STEM Academy student of the month, introduced Dr. Levett, who then spoke about local individuals and groups who labor that their neighbors have safe homes, enough to eat, access to health care. "Dr. King's 'Letter' saw that we are tied together in a single garment of destiny."

At program's end bluebirds were flying as Polote sang "Somewhere over the Rainbow." And when the audience linked arms and swayed to "Lift Every Voice and Sing," it felt like the charm bracelet was unbroken.

Mellencamp wrote, "I cannot forget the people who love me." And on Tybee that day parade marchers and those who cheered them on wrote in a notebook, "I can breathe in a small town."

29

Artists Love Tybee Light

Local painters say the sun here shines in a special way. There is a special Tybee light that shows in the water, in sea oats, in turtles, and in bright shiny pennies.

29

Artists Love Tybee Light

Two months ago I wrote about Joe Lawson and his daily ritual of sitting on the beach to watch the sunrise and feed popcorn to his seagull friends. After 105 straight dawns, he was about to wrap up this winter's sojourn and head home to Indiana; so my wife and I dropped by the Tybee Arts Center on March 15 to say goodbye.

Man, did we stumble into a painters' festival, with sunshine bouncing off the walls and the easels and a roomful of smiles. Every Monday and Friday Joe attends the Open Painting Studio led by Denise Elliot-Vernon. It turned out that this Friday was his birthday.

It was the Ides of March, but there was nothing to beware; quite the opposite, this was something like a family potluck lunch. We arrived just when everyone was putting down their brushes and pick-

ing up their forks to eat and to celebrate the good times that they had shared with Joe.

There was togetherness and hospitality in the room, and I immediately learned how generous the group was too. Sandra Menendez showed me some of the paintings that they were donating to the April 11th Martinis and Masterpieces gala to benefit St. Vincent's Academy. I liked hers: one a moody marsh scene; the other an abandoned country store and gas pump overrun by wildflowers.

Nancee Rubin's painting "Three in a Row" seemed tailored for the upcoming event. It showed three large martini glasses with oversized lemon peels; plenty of vitamin C and anti-inflammatories in those pigments. Joe's own entry "Mending Old Glory" was a lovely close-up of a soldier's hands holding a frayed American flag.

Cathy Lewis showed me "Brother Ben," a feisty rooster that had chased her husband years ago after he tried to show their young son that there was nothing to fear. Vernon's love of utilitarian objects with weight and substance showed in her "Rusty Chock" on a boat's rub rail.

Each painting was personal but also seemed to have been nurtured by the supportive spirit of the group. Menendez was working from an old family photograph: a rear view of a diaper-less crawling baby alongside a golden retriever, both watching the water from a wooden dock. The infant was her grandson, to whom she will give the painting for his upcoming high-school graduation. I had to agree with the other artists that the light on his hiney was just right.

I returned three days later for the Monday class and spoke with Joanne Curran, Denise Titus, and Kathryn Newland. Curran was working on a watery

Impressionist scene. She has been coming to the class for three years when she winters here from Albany, New York. Her first year she painted downtown scenes and the arched oak branches that seem to hallow like church vaults over Savannah streets. Last year she concentrated on the Tybee lighthouse and beach swings.

I was intrigued when she said that this was the first year she painted a person. It turns out that it was Joe, striking a pose of a generic figure bending over picking up some coins. She explained that she has a friend in Birmingham who regularly pens reflections on everyday wonders, entitled "Bright Shiny Pennies." She is going to surprise him with the painting of Joe when she passes through on her way home next month.

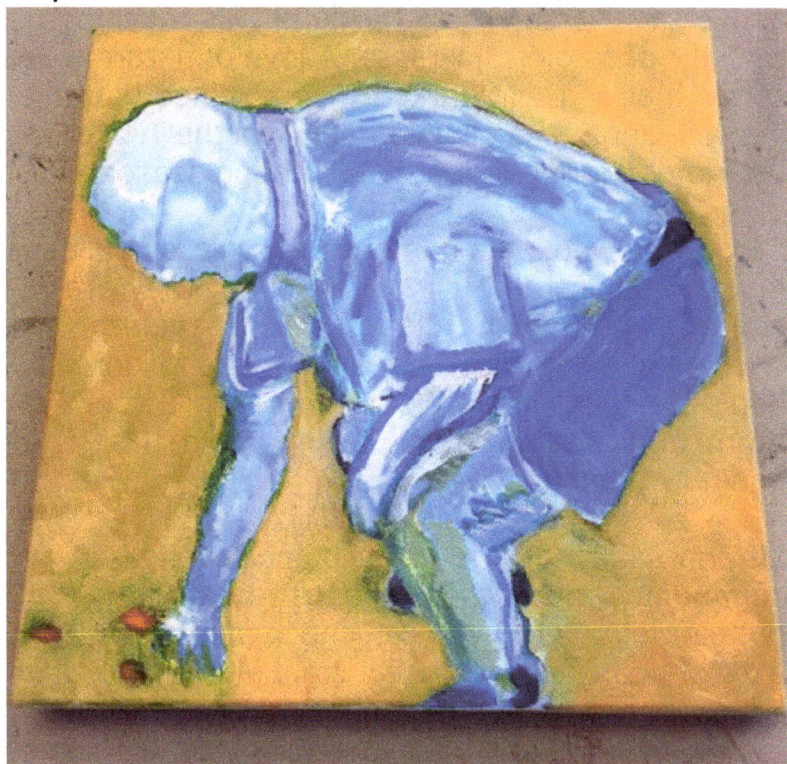

Titus was starting on a golden and lavender sky above the marsh, while Newland was touching up the gills of a colorful wrasse. A love of nature wove through all of their work. Titus explained that she, Vernon, and Lewis all volunteer with the Tybee Turtle Project during loggerhead nesting season.

Vernon showed me a damaged fiberglass public-art loggerhead statue "Terra Turtle" that they are restoring – putting the globe of Earth again on her back, in keeping with Native American folklore. Tybee's Dept. of Public Works and Main Street Program are committed to getting Terra positioned again in Memorial Park.

Vernon said that she loves being involved in the community and does not want to be an artist in a bubble. In my view you can check that off. There is a lot of heart and reciprocal creativity in that Open Studio.

Whether it's a baby or a turtle crawling, Joe picking up pennies, fishermen on the pavilion or in the surf, sea oats or rusty boat gear, there is a quality to Tybee light. Wavelengths that carry a freshness and clear-eyed optimism, onto brushes, onto canvas, and into a wider world.

30

The Lonely Lighthouse

Built in 1848 the little Cockspur Lighthouse at the eastern, oceanmost tip of Fort Pulaski, has weathered hurricanes and cannonballs. Now dedicated friends are trying to save her from the punishing wakes of massive ships.

The Lonely Lighthouse

On April 11, 1862, federal cannons were raining destruction onto Cockspur Island's Fort Pulaski. Confederate forces surrendered the fort that day after a withering 30-hour barrage. Fired from Tybee, the cannonballs travelled in an arc that passed over and spared the Cockspur Lighthouse and its keeper's dwelling.

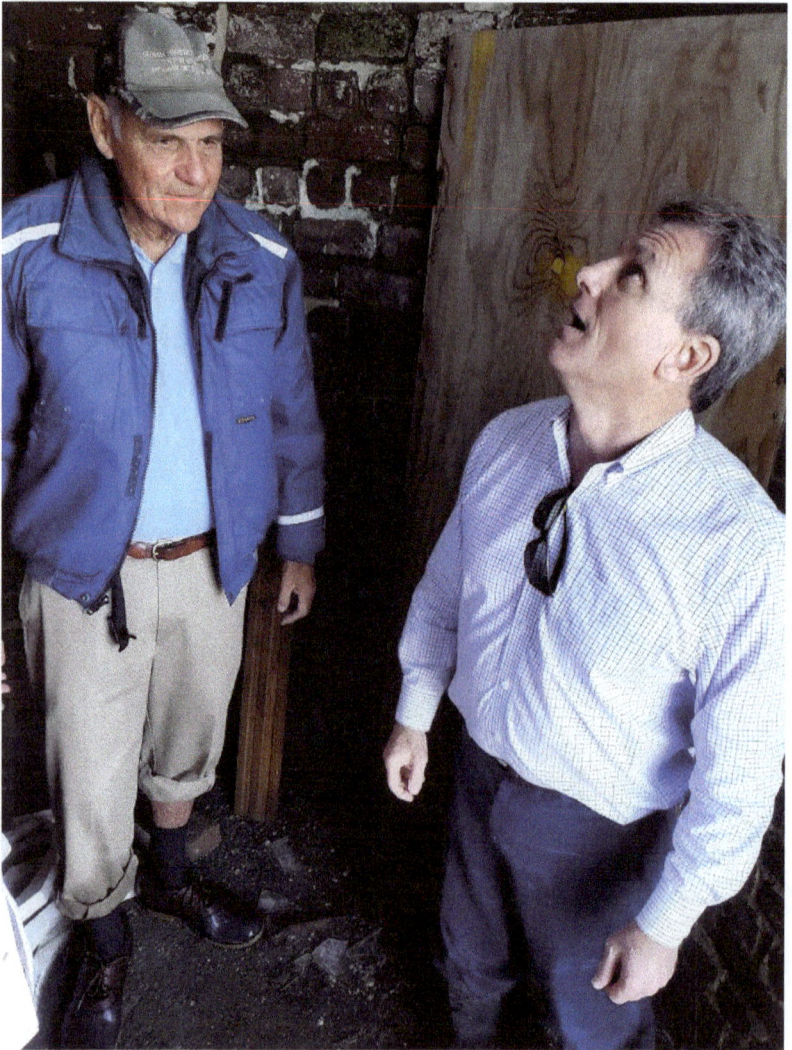

On April 11, 2019, the little lighthouse got a friend-lier federal visit. Congressman Buddy Carter and concerned local citizens motored from Captain Mike's Dolphin Tours' dock on Lazaretto Creek to the small islet on which the lighthouse sits.

On board were members of the Friends of Cockspur Lighthouse, the director of the Tybee Island Histor-ical Society, the superintendent and staff from Fort Pulaski National Monument. The day was clear but breezy; so it took careful maneuvering and some weight-shifting for Captain Allen Lewis to get us all off at a good spot in the shallow water, mud, and oyster shells.

Rep. Carter gamely tromped through the mud in anticipation of getting up close to and inside the historic lighthouse. "I have seen it standing as a welcome to Tybee for many years, but getting close to it made me feel like I was truly part of history. You are inspired to know that you're on the same terrain on Cockspur as John Wesley in 1736; Robert E. Lee on his first assignment in 1830; and Florence Martus, the Waving Girl, who was born there in 1868."

Park Service preservation worker Mark Waldhauer unbolted the door to the lighthouse, and everyone eagerly stepped inside. In the soft, cool light Friends co-founder John Wylly pointed out the graceful interior curvature and the sturdy brick stairway. Carter marveled, "It is nothing short of awesome. I can't imagine what it was like when it was being built in 1848 and rebuilt after a hurricane in 1855, the engineering and construction feats, the challenges of moving bricks and supplies."

Outside Carter had many questions as Pulaski's Facility Manager Emily Harte described the enormous timber pilings and grillage that form the foundation of the lighthouse, and the successful efforts of the past in halting the damage by wood-boring shipworms. He was very interested in details of the repointing of the Savannah-Gray bricks and of the appropriate white paint for the lighthouse exterior.

Wylly explained his shock over a decade ago when he noticed how suddenly the Spartina grass and oyster beds alongside the lighthouse had disappeared. "The currents of the South Channel had shifted, and the sand and mud were sucking out; the whole lighthouse foothold was in danger."

Fellow Tybee resident Capt. Harvey Ferrelle, who runs Sweet Lowland Tybee Tours, had noticed the same thing, that the lighthouse might soon topple into the sea. She faced a threat from her north too - the punishing wakes of massive ships travelling up the North Channel on their way to the Georgia Ports.

With support from Tybee lighthouse preservationist Cullen Chambers the Friends group was formed. Working with the Park Service, Carter's predecessor Congressman Jack Kingston secured $1.5 million in 2012, and the Corps of Engineers built a breakwater of granite boulders, over 5400 tons worth.

Ferrelle says, "That breakwater saved her. Were it not for that breakwater, she would not be standing today." Now the Friends are advocating for broadening the breakwater and repairing the South Jetty that flanks the shipping channel.

The little lighthouse guided ships into port via the South Channel until 1909 when larger ships began using the deeper North Channel and her light was extinguished. Ferrelle notes, "She was a beacon for many years; she played an indispensable role in growing our port; we cannot forget that and abandon her now."

Rep. Carter is already a co-sponsor of HR 2584, the National Park Service Legacy Act, which will direct more funding to maintaining historic buildings like the lighthouse. Leaving Cockspur April 11 he said, "You can count me in. I'm joining the Friends, not just in spirit but in action. It's on us. Local people who care have to become and stay involved."

The Friends group is in for the long haul, the long voyage. Their Facebook page posts beautiful photos almost daily. Their website has stunning historical photos. Videos by Michael Jordan and GPB's Sharon Collins capture the coastal magic. The drone footage shows a dizzying pelican-eye view.

Leaving the Cockspur lighthouse after his own view from her upper window, new Friends member Carter said, "I have a lot of irons in the fire, but only one lighthouse."

31

Thoreau on Tybee

Tybee's most famous calligrapher thinks, writes, and draws like Henry David Thoreau. Whether he is writing about a bird or drawing the bird, it flows off his pen with easy grace.

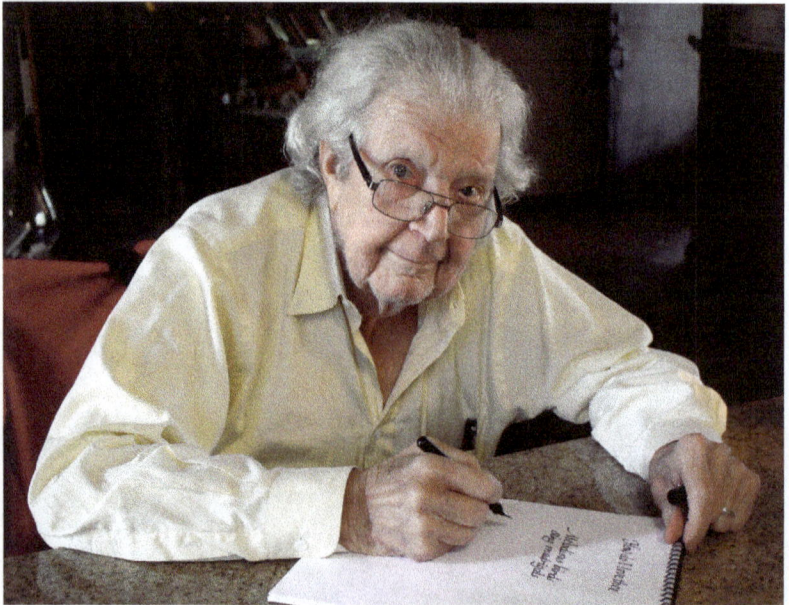

31

Thoreau on Tybee

The dark letters seem to drop down onto the page, forming a procession from left to right, following a careful pattern and taking shape on the parchment like a line of grackles. Arranged by an unseen hand, the letters form a sensation and a thought that capture the spirit and the swagger of the Lowcountry boat-tailed bird.

Boattailed Grackle

Mallory Pearce

That describes the experience of watching calligrapher Mallory Pearce effortlessly write a sentence describing the iridescent blue, purple, and green hues of boat-tailed grackles as they walk across a golf green. Pearce's calligraphy is as natural to him as cursive is to me.

But, where even I can't decipher my scrawls just hours later, Pearce's writing is timelessly clear and

legible. Years ago Janisse Ray wrote in the fore-
word to his book "The Low Country" that he was
"the Thoreau of Savannah," and included a poem
that she wrote about their first meeting.

Most people on Tybee have Pearce's book, which
is full of natural history on every plant and animal that you encounter in coastal marshes and for-
ests. The descriptions and the illustrations are very
much in the vein of Thoreau.

I did not know how much Pearce was like Thoreau
until I visited him last week to have him design
an invitation because of his calligraphy skills. He
showed me the journals that he has kept for a lifetime, and they look like Thoreau's, not only in the
content but also in the script.

Pearce not only loves nature but also the art of
forming letters, the art of inking the words onto
the paper. He keeps calligraphy pens in his breast
pocket like most people keep ballpoints. His act of
writing is as mindful as it gets.

Young Green Heron at Pond

Mallory Pearce

I was surprised to learn that Pearce never learned to write in cursive or to use a typewriter. Until he took up calligraphy in his twenties, he wrote in school and college in "joined manuscript," as rapidly as most people write in cursive.

He showed me different styles of scripts and borders, from Renaissance to Celtic. The graceful italic or chancery-style calligraphy would be familiar to medieval monarchs. The Irish-style calligraphy is something that monks of St. Patrick or St. Brendan would recognize.

He illustrated for me the differences between chisel point and flexible point calligraphy. He easily replicated John Hancock's signature for me, and he wrote out a sentence of the Declaration of Independence in Thomas Jefferson's hand. He wrote a few lines of "Tom Sawyer" in Mark Twain's handwriting, which he had learned for a Twain documentary.

As Shakespeare he penned "How do I love thee?" In the style of a Biblical scribe he wrote, "To everything there is a season and a time for every purpose under heaven." From Christopher Marlowe's poem "The Passionate Shepherd to His Love," he wrote "Melodious birds sing madrigals."

While he worked on my invitation, he popped a DVD "Writing: Plain and Fancy" into his TV for me to watch. The Disney film narrated by John Houseman with script and calligraphy by Pearce covered the development of writing from ancient times to the present.

Afterward he casually wrote for me some Hebrew text. And some Sumerian cuneiform. And he easily illustrated for me the significance of the Rosetta Stone, writing in both Greek and in hieroglyphics.

I visualize Pearce channeling Henry David Thoreau. They are obviously kindred spirits with keen observations of the natural world. His journals, like Thoreau's, are all handwritten and include his drawings of the scenery, the land and the water, the plants and the animals that fascinate him.

I commented on his text and drawings of marsh hens, and he described an encounter where a mother hen charged him to protect her chicks. His sketch of Otto, the otter that lives in the marsh at Chimney Creek, who Crab Shack owner Jack Flanigan has tamed and feeds fish by hand, would appeal to Thoreau.

Beauty Berry
Callicarpa americana

Pearce's drawings of beautyberry, wild poinsettia, spiderwort, pileated woodpeckers, minks, herons, hawks, and cicadas sing of home to coastal humans. They carry a sense of place, this place, but they feel universal when surrounded by his calligraphy.

I saw in his drawing of the spherical nest of the marsh wren a woven pattern that echoed the pattern of a Celtic knot. And his calligraphy of the Song of Solomon puts age-old truths, in words and image, onto a timeless page.

June 20
A marsh wren sang from a stalk adjacent to its nest: dry brown blades interwoven with green blades at the tips of the cordgrass. The male marsh wren builds many nests to attract a mate. The female will choose one and finish its interior.

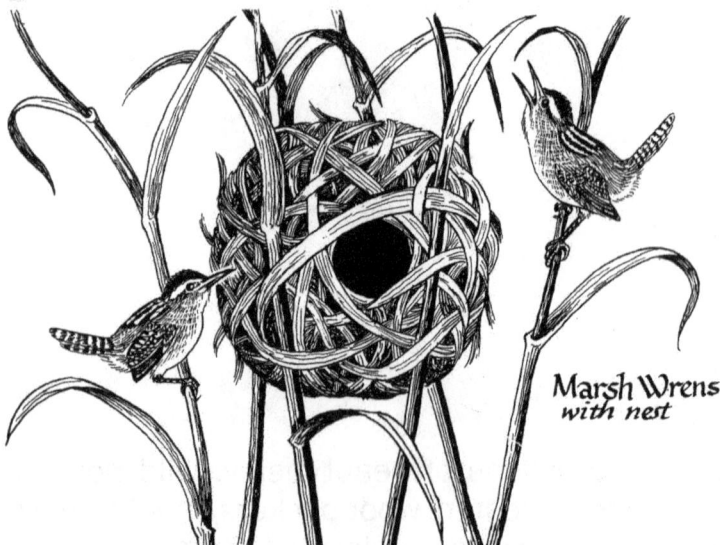

Marsh Wrens
with nest

To talk nature, calligraphy, or Thoreau connect with Pearce at 912-433-1158 or mallorypearce1935@gmail.com.

32

Blues at the Water's Edge

Tybee's big, bad, fedora-wearing blues man Willie Jackson keeps the crowd laughing and tapping. A "big-boned woman" left him with knots all over his head.

32

Blues at the Water's Edge

On Saturday of Memorial Day weekend Tybee's North Beach Grill was full of red, white, and blues. The huge American flag that hung from the lighthouse was blowing in an offshore breeze. And the air of the restaurant deck was full of music and floating fifty-dollar bills.

Willie Jackson and the Tybee Blues Band were playing Muddy Waters' "I'm Your Hoochie Coochie Man." As he sang "I got seven hundred dollars, and don't you mess with me," Jackson held up a bucketful of money and poured it out into the wind. People were scrambling for the flying notes until Jackson said they weren't real.

"It's just play money from the Dollar Store. They have a great exchange rate, and you don't have to keep it in your safe." He said that they used to use real money but had a problem getting it all back.

Even though these bills were fake, lots of fans were tucking them conspicuously into their bathing suit tops.

The audience was laughing and singing along for three hours, and Jackson himself had big reasons to be happy. A month ago he received awards for "Best Blues Song" and "Best Blues Songwriter" at the Indie Music Channel Awards at the Grammy Museum in LA.

I talked with him a few days after the show, and he said what a thrill it was. "The ceremony was held in the Clive Davis Theater. They called out the nominees and then asked for 'the envelope please.' I was just coming offstage for one award when they called me back for the other."

He won for "I'm Your Landlord," a track from his soon-to-be-released album. "It was the first song that we had recorded, so I decided to submit it. I sent it in on the last day to enter the competition, and a week later it was nominated."

He sang it at the North Beach Grill, and for five minutes the crowd laughed and groaned and booed their disapproval over the pompous creep of a landlord speaking to his young female tenant. "I'm your landlord. I appreciate the honey. I'm your landlord, but bring me the money. When you pay me, I have you to thank. 'Cause that's the only thing that I can take to the bank."

Jackson has been writing songs for forty years. The lyrics and the tune come to him at the same time. "I have a sense of humor about common experiences and situations that we've all run into. And I naturally express them in a blues style. Like that knuckleheaded old landlord making himself the victim as he says. 'Don't think I'm soft just because I gave you 52% off.'"

He explained how the song "Sleepin' on the Job," came about when he worked the midnight shift as a chemical operator at Kemira. He was always warning a young co-worker against sleeping on the job. But he morphed the lyrics to be about a man breaking up with his girlfriend for putting no effort into the relationship.

The baleful harmonica and the slow-motion beat seem to capture the night-shift factory atmosphere. The whole phrasing and beat feels like Howlin Wolf, "You're snorin' when you should be workin.' Pack your bags and go."

Playing to a crowd is right in Jackson's wheelhouse. Years back he began playing Sunday nights at the Sand Bar on Tybee in what became the popular "Blues Night" with different musicians joining in.

The blues were never so much fun as at the North Beach Grill. With Jim Simmons on harmonica, Rodney Smith on bass, Zach Jones on drums, and Vincent Jenkins on lead guitar, Jackson sang 28 songs, himself playing congas, maracas, and tambourine.

Jackson always wears a fedora, and some folks in the audience were wearing them too. The cover portrait on his EP "Chosen by the Blues" was done by his wife Carol, an artist and retired special-ed teacher. His daughter Alise is a vocalist at Savannah Arts Academy, and his daughter Patrice is a visual arts major at Armstrong.

When his album "All in the Blues" comes out, I hope that his wife does a sketch inspired by his song "Big Boned Woman." "She buys me gas and tires; she keeps me on the road; she's always cookin' biscuits...She left me in a corner with knots all over my head."

Now that's some old-school blues. Blues from the water's edge.

33

Lost Souls of Lazaretto

Lazaretto Creek takes its name from the quarantine station established there in slavery days. In the photos of SCAD's Nicki Klepper pilings become headstones and troubled waters hold muffled cries.

Lost Souls of Lazaretto

In May I got a new appreciation for the Bible story of Lazarus (John 11: 43-44). Jesus called in a loud voice, "Lazarus, come out!" The dead man came out, his hands and feet wrapped with strips of linen, and a cloth around his face. Jesus said to them, "Take off the grave clothes and let him go."

I attended a photography exhibition at the Drawing Room Gallery. The show, called "Lazaretto," sprang from the "Hidden Histories" collaboration between the Georgia Historical Society and SCAD. A program in which art history students expand on the information on roadside historical markers which surround Savannah.

Student Nicki Klepper delved into the marker that stands near Lazaretto Creek, alongside the Tybee Island loggerhead turtle welcome sign. The story

behind the marker and the name "Lazaretto" so inspired Klepper that she turned her research into her MFA thesis.

Having grown up on Long Island, she often drove to Lazaretto Creek as a break from study and for an atmosphere something like her home. "I spent time there with a sense of nostalgia. I could close my eyes, hear the birds and the talk of shrimpers and boaters, smell the salt air and the marsh, feel the sun and wind on my face. It would take me home. And for my photography, I loved the aesthetic of the place."

"I have some Italian ancestry, so I knew that 'lazaretto' was an Italian word, but until I read the marker, I never knew the gravity of the name." A combination of Lazarus and Nazareth, a hospital in 16th-century Venice, the word came to describe a quarantine station, to shield a population from infectious diseases spread by incoming ships.

"I was shocked to learn that a place that I felt so inviting and comforting could have such a troubling history. I was moved to dedicate this body of work to the lost souls of Lazaretto. Now that I know of them, may they never be forgotten."

When James Oglethorpe founded the colony of Georgia, slavery was banned. When the ban was repealed in 1749 and importation of slaves was allowed, an act was passed authorizing the construction of a lazaretto on Tybee's western tip. But it was not until the 1766 arrival of the ship Maryborrow with 78 Africans kidnapped from the rice coast of Senegambia that lawmakers actually bought the land and built the lazaretto.

"I began to see how culture and memory change over time and how we can forget to remember. Since Lazaretto was the portal through which the slave trade came to Savannah, I felt an impulse to tell its story. I was saddened to think of how many people lost their lives there after a 4-to-6 month voyage packed below deck. Then to be buried in unmarked graves."

Klepper has done a wonderful job stirring the imagination and honoring those who passed through or passed away at the lazaretto. Her signature photo "Pillars in Memoriam" of the concrete pilings of a floating dock is tidal tranquility itself. The water is still; the light is dusk; the pilings transform to headstones.

Her charcoal etching/rubbing of the Lazaretto marker, like an ancient woodcut, conjures up the diagrams of the efficient packing of human cargo. Her photos of marsh plants and flowers resemble botanical prints from the golden ages of

exploration and tie together past and present in the natural world.

Her "Lazaretto Creek at Sunrise" evokes the Gullah-Geechee sense of "dayclean." Her reproduction of an old tourist guide captures the sad truths summarized all too lightly.

Her pinhole camera photo from the floating dock is dreamlike and seems to issue a challenge not to view the past "through a glass darkly." Klepper's "Water Study (Four Seasons)" is a documentation of the time she has spent at Lazaretto. Like Monet's series of paintings of the Rouen Cathedral, it is a testament to her undying affection for this special location and "its richly surprising, yet saddening, history."

I asked Klepper if she thought the Lazarus of "lazaretto" was Mary and Martha's brother who was raised from the dead. Or was he the beggar in the parable of the rich man and Lazarus?

The rich man, suffering in hell, asked Abraham in heaven to send Lazarus, who sat beside him, to dip his finger in water and come across the chasm to cool his tongue. Klepper has dipped her hand and heart into local history and honored forgotten souls bound to waters now far less a chasm.

34

Smoke on the Water

North Atlantic Right Whales are an endangered species that has unique ties to Georgia. Our offshore waters are their calving grounds, and every birth is celebrated all along the coast.

Smoke on the Water

Two Sundays ago there was a big right whale bask-
ing on the grass in front of Tybee's Post Theater.
Fortunately there was no cause for alarm. She had
not beached herself, and she did not need human
help to get her back into the nearby surf.

She was an inflated whale named "Smoke," a mascot of the Marine Science Center, and she was there
for a Whale Week activity featuring filmmakers Liz
Witham and Ken Wentworth. They are producing
"Follow the Journey," a documentary about Georgia's official marine mammal, the North Atlantic
Right Whale.

The Science Center adopted the real-life Smoke in
2012 through the New England Aquarium's Right
Whale Research Program. Her inflated version rep-
resents her size as a newborn in 1996, about 15
feet long and 3000 pounds. Smoke's family tree is

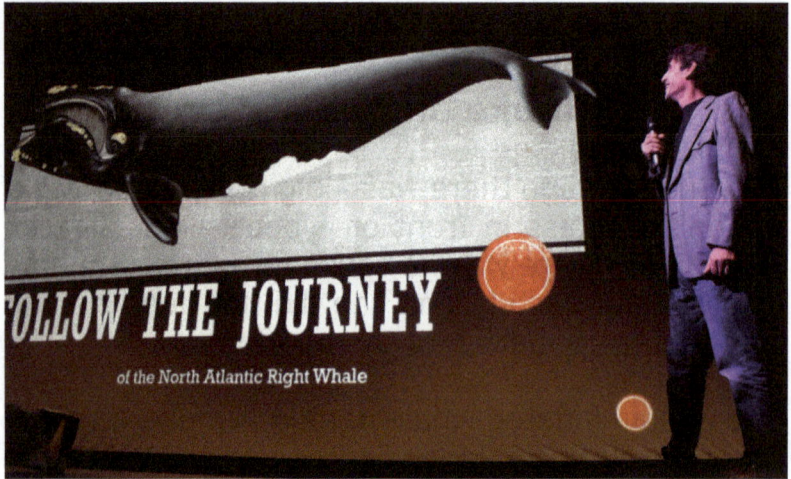

impressive; a replica of her mother "Phoenix" hangs in the Smithsonian. Her grandmother "Stumpy" was called the "Grandmother of Right Whales" by the Aquarium.

Smoke has returned in the winter months three times to the warm waters of Georgia's broad continental shelf. She has given birth to calves in 2007, 2010, and 2014. Georgia Gov. Brian Kemp and all of her fans at the Post Theater are hoping that she returns pregnant again this year, but it's not a sure thing.

Before the filmmakers' presentation Paulita Bennett-Martin of the conservation group Oceana read a proclamation from Gov. Kemp underscoring the state's commitment to the right whales' conservation and the protection of their critical nursery area. He celebrated that last season saw no entanglements or dead whales here.

Entanglements and ship collisions are real dangers. Smoke's grandmother Stumpy was 29 when she died in 2004 off the North Carolina coast after being hit by a passing ship. She was found to be

pregnant with a son who was only weeks from being born in our waters.

Smoke's mother Phoenix survived a fishing-gear
entanglement in 1997, a year after Smoke was
born. Smoke herself survived a life-threatening entanglement injury between August 2002 and April
2003. 85% of right whales show entanglement
scars.

How did Smoke get her name? Researchers can
readily identify right whales by the callosities,
rough skin patches, found on their heads. Every
whale has a different callosity pattern. Smoke was
named because the four patches behind her double
blowholes resemble smoke signals.

The filmmakers are following seven calves over
2000 miles for one year, from their Georgia calving
grounds to the feeding grounds of the Canadian
Maritimes.

There are estimated to be only about 400 right
whales left, so every loss is important. It was
heartbreaking to see photos of an entangled whale

with heavy fishing rope cutting through its baleen and making feeding impossible. And it was sad to see photos of another dead whale with a string of deep chop-chop-chop cuts down his back from a ship's propeller.

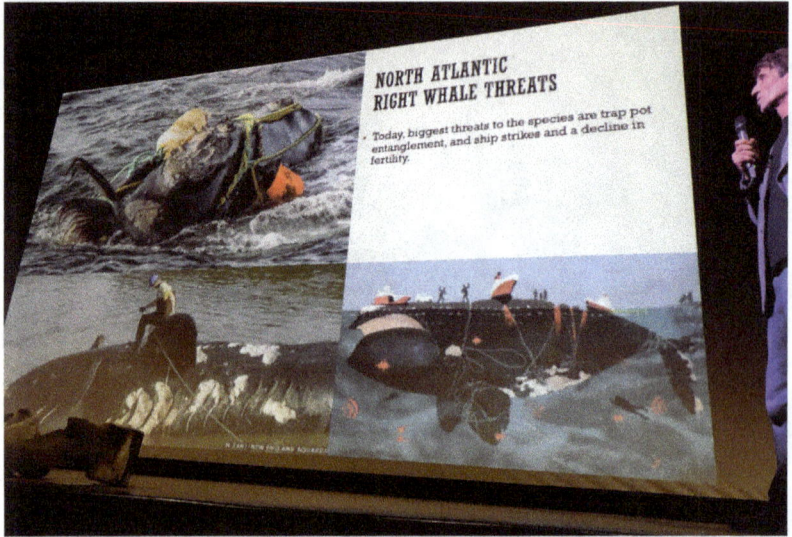

The right whales once had another calving area off Spain, but it was lost after the last prospective mothers were killed. Now governments, researchers, and citizen scientists are determined to save the North American population.

Witham and Wentworth described the broad efforts. Just this January NOAA spotter planes discovered a breeding group of 100 whales off Nantucket. Volunteers with the Marineland Right Whale Project recorded the first Florida mother-calf pair of 2019 with a drone. Their video of the mother and calf swimming peacefully on the glassy sea is a picture of what we hope can forever be. A dart fired from a special crossbow and safely retrieved from the calf will determine its father.

The filmmakers recorded brave volunteers with the Campobello Whale Rescue in the Gulf of St. Lawrence. They met Canadian-US scientists analyzing baleen to figure out what and where the whales are feeding.

They played the 1956 audio of the first recorded right whale sound from a whale named "Scoop" off Martha's Vineyard. He currently is the oldest known living North Atlantic right whale.

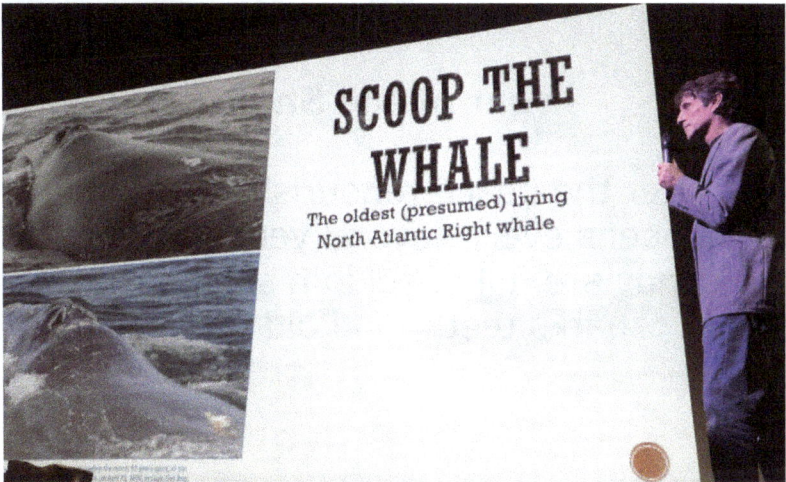

SCOOP THE WHALE
The oldest (presumed) living North Atlantic Right whale

They told the creation story of the Pilgrim-befriending Wampanoag Indians who consider the whales their cousins. Anthropologist Simona Perry taught the audience the Muscogee word for gratitude, spoken to thank the whales for returning.

At the time of the Whale Week program five expectant mother whales had arrived. This is a time of preparation, hopefully to soon be a time of fulfillment. Let's hope, along with Gov. Kemp, that Smoke soon appears.

Maybe, like a good friend of mine says. "She's already here." Now that would be more excellent.

35

Year of the Shell

After the beach renourishment that happens every several years, Tybee's sands are full of seldom seen shells, sharks teeth, and old metal.

35

Year of the Shell

One of my New Year's resolutions is to meet more seagulls. You know, to reach out and reach up, to widen my circle of friends, feathered and not. To step out of my comfort zone and hold pieces of stale bread and soft tortillas in the air and not flinch as the gulls nip my fingers every other time they take them.

It's worth the thrill, and it's one of the simple treats on Tybee in the wake of the winter beach renourishment. The Ring-billed Gulls are teeming, their calls always excited. They are exuberant and vocal as they hover within an easy food toss, their yellow eyes bright and expectant, ready to catch morsels at the top of their arc.

The million-plus cubic yards of sand spread across the beach is a bonanza for shell collectors, shark teeth hunters, and metal detectors. In the last weeks I've seen high and low tech metal detectors, some interesting finds, and some bummers.

While they looked for shells, one Dad's three young sons had cords tied around their waists with horseshoe magnets trailing behind them. When they paused to see what they had "caught," they carefully pulled the cords, like working a hand line so as not to dislodge the crab clinging to the chicken neck. The Dad called it "magnet trolling," and it was good for the boys' imaginations to wonder at the stories behind the rusty nuts, bolts, and bits of "meteorites" that they pulled in.

One day I chatted with two men with metal detectors as they dug deep to uncover a long object that had the signature of dissimilar metals. Sure enough, they eventually uncovered a heavy rusted rudder that was filled with lead for extra weight.

On another day two more guys with metal detectors were digging for a target that "seemed to move" and was pretty confusing in the signals the sensors were picking up. I never ever expected what they dug up. It was, wait for it, a mangled metal detector, "a Y2K model," they said. I guess that, like a frustrated golfer throwing his club into the water hazard, some treasure hunter, about to faint on a sweltering day, had tossed away his trusty electronic bloodhound. You don't just lose a metal detector.

The beach renourishment has thrown up such volumes of shells that almost every beachcomber leaves with a sackful. There are more whelk shells than I have ever seen on Tybee. Many are the classic heavy Knobbed Whelk used by Native Americans as hammers, hoes, and bowls.

There are plenty of the less common whelk shells too: the Channeled Whelk with its smoother silhouette and groove along its whorls; the sleek Pear Whelk; and the Lightning Whelk whose spiral runs counter-clockwise and has its opening on the left-hand side.

Just as interesting as the intact specimens are the many fragments that reveal the inner architecture of the whelks. You see the sturdy twist of the inner columella that looks like the support for a spiral staircase. Coastal Indians valued that core spiral for making beads and jewelry.

In shells, spirals are everywhere. In the multitudes of globular Moon Snails, the slender Olive shells

with their zigzag patterns, the high-spired drill-bit Auger shells. I'm sure that mathematicians walk in Fibonacci spirals instead of grid patterns when they are out collecting.

Among the millions of shells, fossil shark teeth are more plentiful too. So much so that City Arborist Brent Levy has instituted a daily bag limit for them. I don't see the connection between arborists and shark teeth, but he assured me that it is within his purview because it is the Georgia state fossil. Strangely, his own collection seems to be growing like never before.

For Christmas my wife and I got a tide clock from Georgetown Pottery in Maine. The single hand moves around the dial in 12 hours and 25 minutes (half the lunar cycle), so you always know what the tide is doing. Our clock's pattern is two little sanderlings, the shorebirds that skitter along the beach just ahead of arriving and retreating waves, poking the sand for tiny clams. When the tide is low, it's time for beachcombing.

Last week we met a woman with a metal detector rushing to her car. She showed us a Spanish doubloon, pierced like it might have hung around a pirate's neck. She said that she was leaving before the City Arborist might designate it a fossil.

36

Suffering Succulents

Succulents are an easy gardening choice on Tybee. Driftwood and mailboxes make the perfect planters in this arid zone.

36

Suffering Succulents

As Sylvester the Cat, a cartoon character from my formative years, often exclaimed, "Sufferin' succotash." Surprises can be right around your own corner, and timing can be everything.

Just when I was looking to dispose of two old lounge chairs, they appeared on a wanted poster by Tybee artist Lea Lynch. She was asking neighbors for rusted beach chairs for an art installation with a working title of "Seas the Day." My chairs were perfect specimens.

When I added them to the growing heap in Lea's yard, I was taken with the little wooden house that is her family's mailbox. Mail goes into its front door, but its roof is gone, exposing an attic interior that's out of a fairy tale or a dollhouse dream.

It's a miniature attic full of thriving succulents. The little garden was composed of wonderfully arranged aloes and sedums. Their beautiful fleshy whorls and stems were shades of rose, lavender, gray-green, saffron, and jade. They must be a regular joy to the postman.

But the succulents don't stop there. Lea pointed me toward several weathered long pieces of driftwood. The natural crevices and knots in the driftwood are perfect holders for a little soil and lots of succulents. They look like balance beams in a gnome's playground.

Lea said that she has always loved succulents and that they are suited for someone like her with a black thumb. "They are difficult to kill. The more you ignore them, the better they do. The only surefire plants that I've been able to raise are succulents."

The ones in her mailbox are her oldest plants, and she is intrigued with how they change color over time. Whether caused by minerals in the air or water, she's not sure, but they can slowly change from greenish shades of dusky blue, gray, and brown to soft hues of red, orange, and purple.

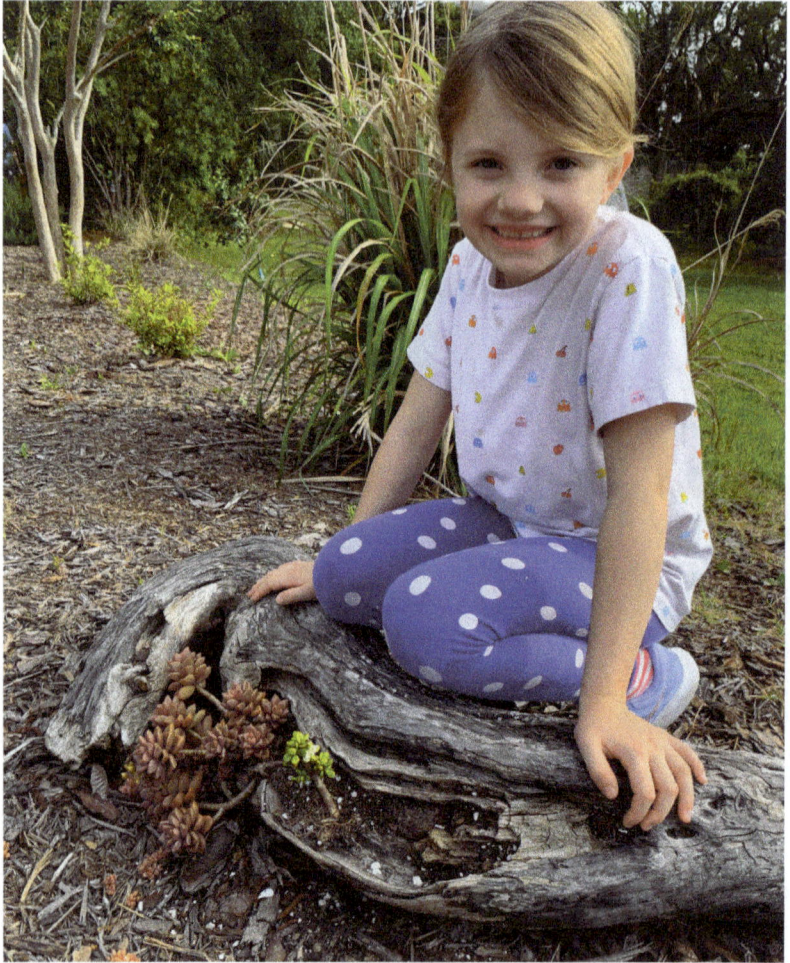

That slow unpredictable shift in their color palette is a continuing discovery. And Lea is also fascinated with how many succulents seem to be visual representation of precise mathematical equations, a harmonious geometry in nature.

Lea didn't know the names of any of her plants. "I'm a visual and textural shopper. There is such variety in succulents. Some have leaves that are flat and velvety; some have a matte finish; some are shiny; each one is a little piece of art."

The idea of placing them in the driftwood and mailbox came from a chance encounter at a plant show with Jessica Gorman. Gorman lives on Burnside Island and is the owner of The Seated Succulent. Her Facebook and Instagram pages are visions of inspiration and tranquility.

Gorman explained how succulents are resilient and easy to propagate. "A cut leaf on a sunny windowsill will sprout little roots in days." She anchors succulents in moss for many of her arrangements, so that they live practically as air plants.

She designs living wreaths and hanging gardens. She's used old railroad lanterns and autumn pumpkins as holders. Her recent Easter designs with palm leaves radiating from a heart of succulents captured the joy of the resurrection.

Lea's neighbor John Eskandari shared some historical insights about her placing succulents in driftwood, a connection to a Victorian practice called "stumpery." He should know. He teaches arborists at the Chicago Botanic Garden.

In stumpery, parts of the forest were brought to the garden. Stumps, limbs, and timber became showcases for ferns, lichens, and mosses. On Tybee Eskandari sees the beach as the forest, with driftwood the perfect support and succulents the perfect fit for an arid zone.

Maybe Tybee's onto something called "driftwoodery." Witness the cactus and succulents Kim Voigt grows in tables her husband Tony has crafted from trees felled by Hurricane Matthew. Witness the driftwood mobiles hanging in Ruth and Doug MacKay's pergola.

Were he an island cat, a sandbur in his paw, Sylvester might nowadays shout, "Sufferin' succulents."

37

Always Time to Yo-Yo

On Tybee, if you need an official timekeeper, Carl Looper is your man. More than the average renaissance man, he's been a bodybuilder, a stilt-walker, a yo-yo champ, a juggler, and a clown.

37

Always Time to Yo-Yo

When I visited Carl Looper on Tybee last week, his parrot Indy greeted me with a friendly, "Welcome, please have a seat." Carl told me that she spoke about fifty words.

About an hour later she chirped again. It sounded like, "Two minutes." I was just processing that phrase when she gave me a cheery, "Your time is up."

I guess I should've seen that coming since Carl is famously the official timekeeper for all of Tybee's pre-election debates and forums. Dressed in a black-and-white referee's shirt, with a whistle hanging from his neck and a board of red-yellow-green colored lights in front of him, he keeps speakers to their time limits.

Carl is a natural for the referee role because of his lifetime of involvement with athletics. He has always been a guy who is "in the arena." He's a Walter Cronkite type of guy you can respect and trust.

As a young man he held numerous national weight-lifting titles and went on to referee. He was on the staff at the 1984 Olympics in Los Angeles. His own photo album looks like it could belong to Charles Atlas.

Or to Clyde Beatty. He's juggled and done acrobatics with the circus. He's competed internationally playing ping-pong. He's set records for round-the-worlds as a Duncan Yo-Yo professional.

Carl is certifiably larger than life. A guy many people have looked up to in the very literal sense. He's performed on stilts as Abe Lincoln and as Uncle Sam, walking entire parade routes while ten-feet tall.

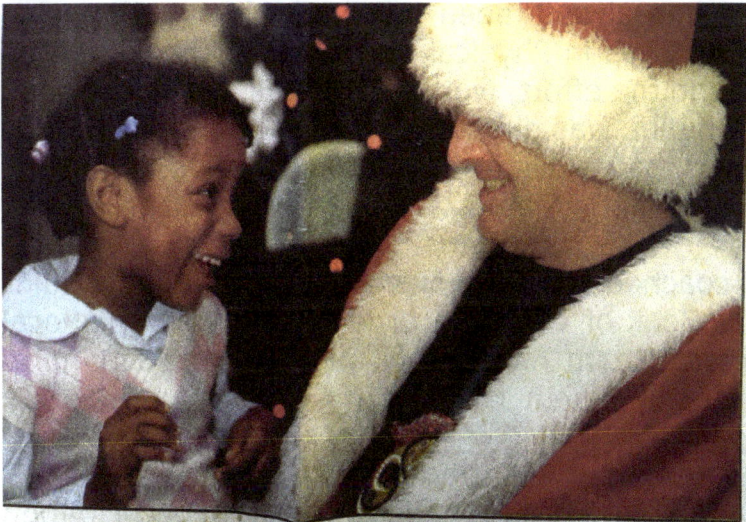

Staff Photo by PETER B. SCHUMACHER

Passing the Word With a Smile

Signing His Christmas Wishes

As St. Patrick he has driven the snakes (green-clad school kids) off the Emerald Isle of Tybee. And his Santa Claus has brought happiness to many a hopeful child.

Carl has always been involved with youth, using his degrees in Physical Education, to help children expend the effort, work on the skill, reach the goal. In Ohio he was director of a Mini-Circus where kids honed their skills to develop innovative gymnastic and acrobatic feats.

He coached a youth unicycle team that set a Guinness Book of World Records height mark. His local unicycle team rode many miles down Savannah's streets on March 17.

Carl and his wife Kathy are both retired Special Education teachers. He helped start local participation in the Special Olympics, and he shared with me

moving stories of the full hearts and bright eyes of kids celebrating their events. He coached many kids with disabilities in wheelchair basketball and soccer.

Everything he's done, he's done with eagerness, exuberance, laughs, and love. Right off the bat on

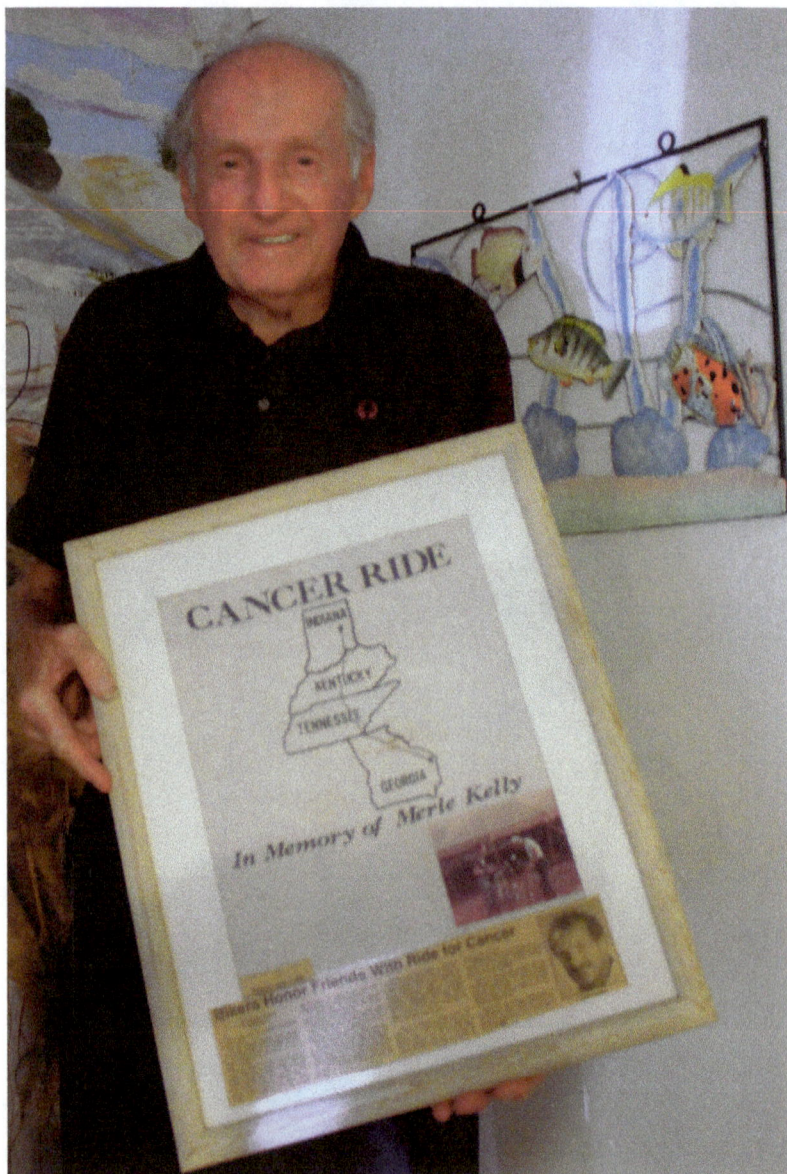

my visit, Indy the parrot pointed me toward a 1986 Savannah Evening Press front-page article with Carl and his fiancé Kathy applying for their marriage license dressed as clowns.

They had just finished performing for a group of special-needs children and, still in costume and make-up, stopped by Probate Court. The magic of clowns and the circus is woven through Carl's life. From the age of ten he worked as a circus hand when it came to town.

He has been a member of the Shriners Clown Unit for fifty years. "It's love to the rescue, transforming children's lives. Never underestimate the muscles used to smile."

There don't seem to be any muscles that Carl hasn't used. He's run three marathons. He's bicycled across Georgia five times. He biked a thousand miles in six days from Indiana to Georgia with two friends to raise money for cancer research after losing a friend to the disease.

This November the Shriners are bringing a circus to Savannah. Carl will bring his circus too. He has a forty-foot scale-model miniature circus with 20,000 parts that he built. It will be on display at the Alee Temple.

Carl will be the friendliest guy there. Maybe as a clown, maybe as a referee, maybe as a ringmaster. Some people just go through life that way.

38

Feathers and Fur

The Nextdoor social network on Tybee ties together two-legged and four-legged (and winged) citizens.

Feathers and Fur

Back in the late 1960's Scott McKenzie's lyrics filled the air and captured a wistful spirit. "If you're going to San Francisco, you're going to meet some gentle people there."

The same might be said about the folks on Tybee Island. It does look like it will be a summer of love, but the lyrics to this song write themselves as they tumble easily off the Lost and Found posts on the Nextdoor social platform.

Last week there was a bright note when John and Sherry Crowell posted a splashingly blue photo of a found parakeet. John had been in their yard on Spanish Hammock when he heard a bird singing in the tree above him. He spoke a little parakeet; so it hopped down the limb, onto his arm, and then onto his head.

Sherry put some of their wild bird seed onto a saucer, and the little guy took to it like he was famished. She then took him inside to a quiet room and, hoping to reunite him with his owner, posted his photo on Nextdoor.

Several Tybee folks offered to adopt him. Belinda Flanigan brought over a spare cage from the menagerie that she has at her Crab Shack restaurant.

The Crowell's grandchildren in California have named the little budgie Tweety-Bird and Pickles and wish they would keep him. Until his owner turns up, he's being adopted by another kind local. When I dropped by to see him, he was enjoying nibbles of banana and apple in addition to his millet.

Just up the road in Spanish Hammock another nice story was unfolding, again via the channel of Nextdoor. On the same day that Pickles whistled in the Crowells' yard, a lost cat showed up at sundown on the third-floor deck of Jeff and Linda Koenings.

They posted a photo of the crisp black-and-white cat in a thoughtful pose on the deck. Jeff thinks the deck's height may give her a sense of security. She has come to sleep there every night but wants to stay out of their reach.

A few days ago Jeff was walking their dog Cooper when Carol Porterfield, who lives a good quarter-mile away, was putting a flyer in their mailbox. She was searching for her cat Priss. That's the cat – unmistakable with its striking orca markings.

Now as soon as Priss returns at nightfall, Jeff will call Carol to come sweet-talk her home. She belonged to Carol's mother-in-law who moved into assisted living; so last fall Priss moved as well, in with the Porterfields.

LOST CAT

My nine year old cat got out of the house on Sunday May 10th. She is not a friendly cat and will be scared since she has been an inside only cat.

Please call if you see her. Her name is Priss.

Thanks

She's a 9-year-old inside cat, but she wandered out last week and disappeared. Carol was searching all over Spanish Hammock and was amazed to discover that Priss had covered so much ground, even crossing a marshy creek.

Priss' story makes me reminisce about how I got my cat Frank. Three years ago Deb Baber posted a persuasive "Pet Needs a Home" written in the first person.

"Hello, my name is Frank. I am a little older guy, and I have been neutered. My owner had to go to live with some people in a nursing home. I am missing some teeth, but I am a lover. I use the litter box and get along with other cats. I am lonely right now, and I would be a good companion for anyone. As you can see by my photo, I am quite good looking.

"Message my friend Deb if you need or want a furry friend. I am your guy." Well, I soon adopted Frank and felt like an island hero when Deb posted "I Have a New Dad!"

I posted photos of Frank in his new home for all the people who had been pulling for him. I look forward now to photos of the further exploits of Pickles and Priss this summer, maybe "with flowers in their hair."

39

Patron Saint of Felines

Cats have nine lives, and feral cats can have nine rough ones. Tybee's Marie Rodriguez has labored one human lifetime being a feline comfort animal.

39

Patron Saint of Felines

On Tybee, if the conversation turns to cats, there is a probability that the name Marie Rodriguez will come up. If the conversation turns to feral cats, it's a certainty.

Over the years the quality of life for at least a thousand cats has been a blessing from Marie Rodriguez. She is self-deprecating and often describes herself, "I'm that crazy cat lady." In her case it is indeed a local term of endearment.

Many of us are seeking her canonization as St. Marie. She is an inspirational angel of mercy, ceaselessly working for the health and welfare of the four-legged furry creatures that share our island world.

She has been in the veterinary business her whole life, but stepped into the cat spotlight in 2006. She took her mother Mimi to a local Wheel of Fortune audition, but Marie was the exuberant one they picked for the show.

Tybee had a cookout fundraiser to send Marie, her mother, and daughter to California, but Marie automatically felt the event should benefit a non-profit as well. She chose the Milton Project, a program to spay and neuter both feral and community cats. It took its name from a kitten named Milton who was saved after it hit the railing atop the Talmadge Bridge when someone tried to toss him from the car to the water below. His survival inspired Marie and the program.

Like a lot of Marie's experiences, her Wheel appearance was unusual. She was introduced by Pat Sajak as "the flea Queen of Savannah," because of her vast veterinary knowledge of those minute pests. Then the judges had to pause one game to replay the tapes because her Southern pronunciation of "He said, she said" was tough for them to discern. She was cleared.

In something that I think was consistent with her benevolent pet advocacy, she solved "Philanthropist." When she won a trip to Venice after solving "Romantic Gondola Ride," she did not take any cats as Sajak suggested, but took her thrilled and deserving mother instead.

Marie does not think of the plight of feral and community (domestic abandoned) cats in the abstract. She feels their pain. She knows their stories and is involved in many ways.

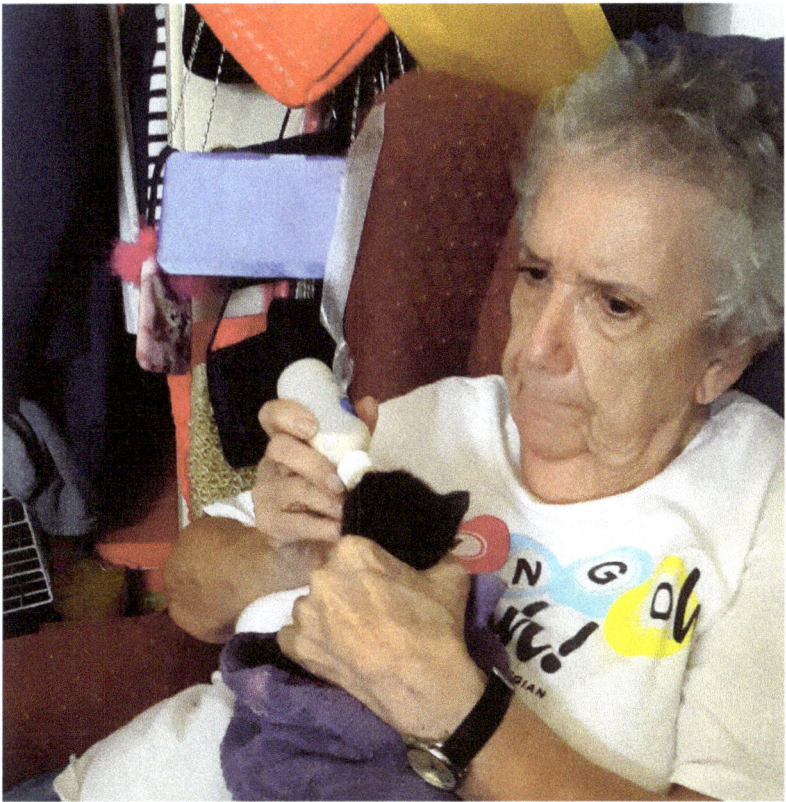

She has worked for the all-volunteer Islands Feral Cat Project which serves all of Savannah and helps the sick and injured feral/community cat population. She volunteers with One Love Animal Rescue, donating her time and money to transport and spay/neuter cats in their care.

She volunteers whole-heartedly with the Humane Society for Greater Savannah. "Whatever they need me to do: folding laundry, organizing rooms, picking up donations, running the cotton candy machine at the Doggie Carnival, fostering. People often ask me why I foster, and my best answer is that I am saving a life. By fostering and adopting out a cat or kitten you are allowing another to be saved."

She is right now fostering a Mama cat and three kittens. Mama and her two brothers were dumped one year ago as juveniles. A person who feeds the feral cats at that location included the three. No one knew that they were not fixed.

Then in April Mama had four kittens. Marie is fostering them and will get them all adopted in another month. What a hard life Mama has had this past year. Once loved, then dumped in the wild. "She is so loving. She has let me vaccinate her, deworm her, and trim her nails."

Inspired by Marie my wife and I are fostering three little kittens from HSGS right now. After the Brady Bunch, we've named them Marsha, Marsha, Marsha. It's a joy to hear the little tick tick tick against a constant background purr as they suck their bottles. To see the look of devotion in their little blue eyes. To start them on a lifetime of happy days.

40

Don't Show Your Butt

Tybee's beaches stay clean and scenic because lots of locals do regular beach sweeps to pick up litter. They fight dirty.

Don't Show Your Butt

The Facebook profile photo for Fight Dirty Tybee gets your attention. It's one word written on the beach. It's not what you usually see in script drawn in the sand with a finger or stick. It's not somebody's name or "Peace" or "Love" or curvy lines that will wash away with the next tide.

The word is "Quit," and it's formed in block letters with piles of cigarette butts. Butts that were litter just hours before. Butts picked up by people who love the unspoiled beauty of the beach.

Every Sunday evening or Monday morning from spring to fall there is a beach clean-up hosted by the grass-roots group Tybee Clean Beach Volunteers. They scour the beach for all the litter left behind by weekend crowds.

It's straightforward work that is instantly rewarding. You make an immediate environmental and
aesthetic difference. I joined the effort June 1 at
the pavilion at 9:30 AM.

Tim Arnold and the TCBV team were signing people in. Each volunteer got two pieces of equipment. That's all you need - a bucket for one hand,
a reacher/grabber for the other. The bucket has a
painter's cup hung inside it for cigarette butts; the
rest of the bucket is for everything else.

As I looked out over the already-hot shimmering
beach, the volunteers were silhouetted against the
glare of the water, and they reminded me of Picas-
so's famous black-and-white sketch of Don Quix-
ote. The Lyric Stage of Dallas produced Man of La
Mancha last year, and their poster featured that
image against a background like the Tybee summer sun.

These volunteers, however, were not on horse-
back, using lances to tilt at windmills. They were

on foot, using grabbers to pick up butts. Kansas visitor Denise Duerksen said, "A clean beach is not an impossible dream."

After the morning's sweep I spoke with Tim Arnold, and he gave me some stats on the two-hour clean-up. He was happy with the turnout of 58 people for their first "post-Covid" sweep. The equipment they supplied was sanitized. The team did the litter sorting afterward, so that volunteers could keep good distancing on that step.

"We get a lot of families who help," said Arnold. I saw exuberant groups like Kristin Herbert and her three sons Alexander, Anthony, and Andrew. Danielle Wiltie and her young son Asher were eagerly darting their grabbers and enjoying the cool action of the pinchers.

Susan Hoang was shepherding a group of kids from Talahi and Whitemarsh Islands as they dueled on and off with their grabbers. A pair of students from Spelman College majoring in Environmental Science said that they really appreciated the eco-friendly buckets.

Arnold said that the EcoSmart buckets themselves are made from recycled plastic. "And we use Ettore grabbers that are easy to rebuild. You can pick up 200 butts and not break a sweat."

"We try to be a zero-waste beach sweep." They don't just collect trash and send it to landfill. They use elbow grease and willpower to find a recycling home for all the litter streams.

Arnold joked that Terracycle, where they send cigarette butts, had called recently to ask if there was a problem because they had not gotten any recent shipments. "It's because we're holding about 100,000 behind the Tybee Marine Science Center to be used for an educational display. Terracycle breaks butts down to plastic for plastic pallets, ash and tobacco to compost, etc."

"Local corporate groups who help us don't come with single-use water bottles, individually-packaged snacks, or disposable gloves. Instead they bring Igloo coolers, sturdy reusable bottles, personal gardening gloves, bananas and apples that we compost."

"We get lots of local help from Boy Scouts, Girl Scouts, students from New Hampstead and Heard and our colleges. Vacationing tourists are glad to discover us and to participate. They tell me, 'We're happy to help keep a clean beach. That's why we came.'"

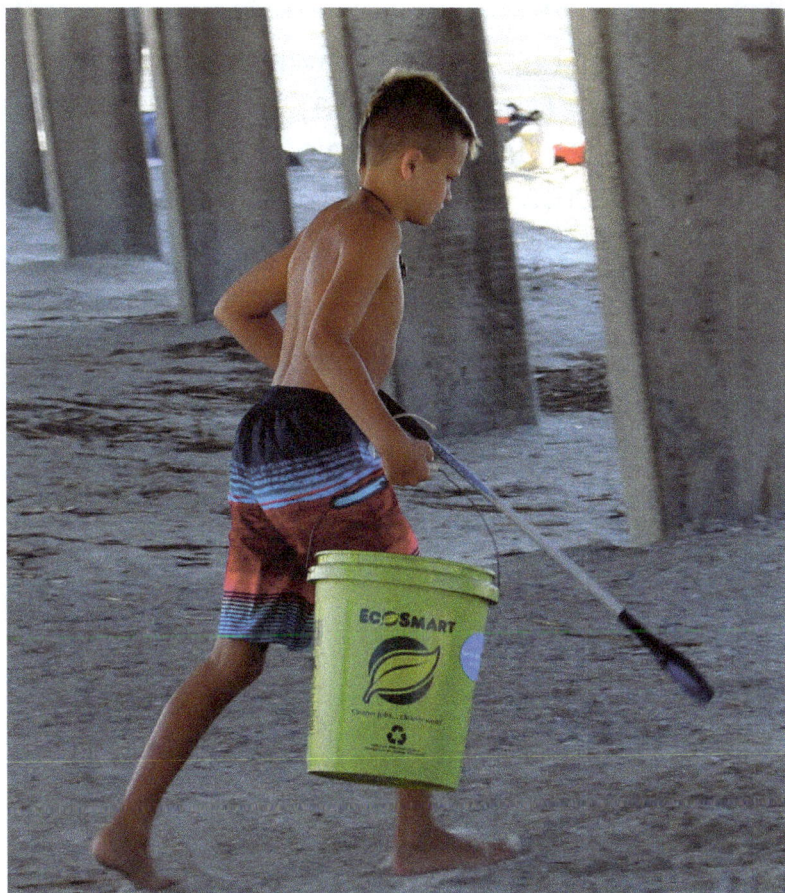

41

Born for Grease

"If your car breaks down, take it to Freddie's." The air is free; the dog treats are free; and Freddie's Garage has protected and served families on Tybee since 1946.

41

Born for Grease

In July, ahead of our son coming to visit from Nebraska, I took my wife's Honda over to Freddie's Garage on Tybee to check the air in the tires and the spare. Freddie's is always several rows deep with parked cars waiting for service.

Service writer Laura Leonard told me to just pull up as close as I could and that the air hose should reach. She handed me a pressure gauge to use. With my weak automotive background (and knees) it took me a half hour to finish the job. When I returned the gauge and asked what I might owe, Laura said, "No charge, come on by any time."

Well, my wife brought the car back a week later. She went to use the car and heard a rattling noise underneath. After she asked our son if he knew what might be the cause, he said that he had not heard the noise, but that it might stem from a drive through Bonaventure Cemetery.

The day earlier he and his girlfriend had taken two other friends on a tour of the cemetery, and he might have, sort of, scraped a thick oak root on a cautious slow-speed drive. Hmmm.

Freddie's young mechanic Gavin Buker put the Honda on the lift and fixed a broken bracket and loose heat shield. My wife waited inside, laughed and chatted with Laura, and soaked up the home-town garage ambience. Laura's husband Roger is the head mechanic, and our dog growled at him when he stepped inside. My wife apologized, but he said not to worry and got out a generous supply of dog biscuits.

The bill was an unbelievably low $10. My wife said that she felt like giving a tip and told me, "You should write about Freddie's."

So here we are. Last week I visited with Freddie Anderson and learned more about this bonafide Tybee institution. It's named after Freddie's dad. The family moved to Tybee in 1946 when Freddie was one year old. The business was initially a filling station and fuel oil dealer.

Those were the days of full service. As kids, Freddie and his brothers helped out, standing on stools to reach and clean car windshields. When he turned 18, Freddie went to work full time at the garage, and he was the only mechanic until Roger came aboard in 2004.

He's proud the business has a reputation for service and dependability. He said that, besides locals and tourists, folks from Wilmington Island and Savannah bring their cars to Freddie's. "Lots of people want only Roger to work on their cars."

Freddie showed me the old cash register his dad bought. It still works and makes a classic ding when the drawer pops open. He showed me the heavy wooden stand that holds the mechanic work logbook. His son made that in high-school shop class and asked Freddie to keep it until he got settled. "He's retired now, so I guess that he's getting close to being settled."

When I visited with Laura, she said that she loves all the old artifacts in the office and garage. She

pointed out the old whetstones, the shop manuals, the chess set made of nuts and bolts by Roger who really enjoys the game.

She grew up in New England small towns. "Tybee reminds me of my upbringing. When people here say, 'How are you doing?' they really want to know."

There is a definite family feel to Freddie's, at the personal and community level. Freddie's wife Cathy was town librarian for many years. Laura gives stuffed animals from her collection to the police; they give them to little kids to comfort them during long traffic stops.

While I was there, city council member Monty Parks came in to pay for his oil change. It was $30, and he tipped an additional $10. "I don't trust anybody but Freddie's to change my oil." With a maternal touch, Laura admonished him to bring it in next time when it was due.

And like a proud mother, she told me how she hopes there is a big Freddie's celebration next year when the family business turns 75.

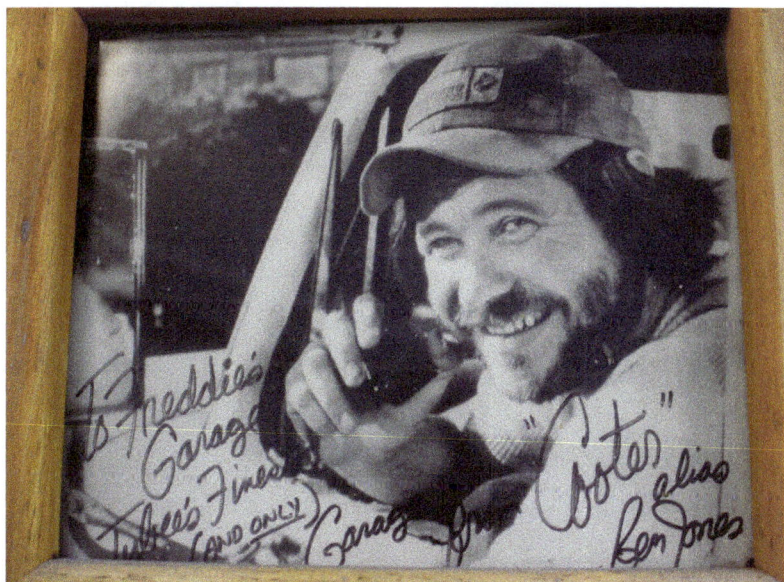

42

Addy's Excellent Adventure

A little loggerhead sea turtle hatchling found in a motel wastebasket becomes a star. After beefing up at the TIMSC aquarium, she is ready to flex her flippers.

Addy's Excellent Adventure

Addy the loggerhead sea turtle lives in an 800-gallon tank at the current Tybee Island Marine Science Center next to the pavilion. She's just over two years old and is about to take the longest trip of her life.

It's not to the open ocean yet; that will happen next summer. Addy's upcoming trip will be only three miles, but it's pretty much a passage from the 20th to the 21st century. She will be the first animal to be transferred from the current center on the Strand to the new one at Tybee's North End. The current center at the South End has operated for 30 years in an apartment-sized building that first served as a police and lifeguard station. The dedicated educators at that humble facility have opened the coastal world to a million visitors.

The new center is the result of fifteen years of planning and fervent support by the Tybee community. It is a state-of-the-art beauty, both inside and outside. I can imagine the impact the staff will have with seven classrooms, a 3500-sq. ft. exhibit gallery, and the views of the fort, the lighthouse, the dunes, and the sea.

Addy will love the spaciousness of her new 5000-gallon tank. It came in four very heavy sections that were unloaded and prepped for assembly by the Tybee Island Fire Department. Thirty years from now Addy might start returning the favor.

She may do that by laying her own eggs on this beach where she was born. I visited Addy in her current digs last week, where curator Chantal Audran spoke about her like a proud parent. "She's a survivor." She and five other hatchlings made national news in July 2018 when they were rescued by an alert housekeeper from a wastebasket at the Admiral's Inn.

They had been taken off the beach on the night they hatched by a couple who was not aware that loggerheads are a federally-protected species. Her siblings were expeditiously released by the Center staff, and Addy was kept to be raised and displayed at the Center to educate the public about logger-heads.

Audran explained that Addy has grown faster than any turtle that they have raised. She gets fed 2%-5% of her body weight daily. She started out weigh-ing 16 grams and is now a whopping 45 pounds.

She eats fresh blue crabs and jellyfish, "shrimp-si-cles," and a custom gelatin blend of kale, carrots, shrimp, squid, and fish. Audran said that the shrimp and squid come from Capt. J.B. Riffle of the Ag-nes Marie. "J.B. has always been a supporter who brings us unusual specimens that he catches in his shrimp trawls, from octopuses to invasive Asian ti-ger shrimp."

One of the new Center's outside exhibits will be a full-scale copy of the Agnes Marie by master

boat-builder Rusty Fleetwood. It will sit beside a Blackbeard Island-themed children's playspace. A film of shrimping aboard the Agnes Marie will be one of many coastal-culture interpretive exhibits inside.

Also outside will be life-sized mother and calf right whale flukes that dive under the center's main entrance. Life-sized models of the five species of sea turtles that visit Georgia beaches will scramble up a dune face.

Inside is a sky loft with views of Calibogue Sound and the shipping channel. It has software to identify ships with live real-time vessel tracking. There will be a ship pilot simulator for visitors to have a try at the critical work Savannah pilots perform in safely guiding ships from the sea to the port and back.

Through the generosity of the city of Tybee, the Fleetwood family, the Makel family, and IKEA, the Center has raised $6.2 million that has funded construction. Now the Tybee Island Marine Science Center Foundation is conducting a campaign to raise the $1.3 million needed to fully obtain the exhibits and displays that will make the Center truly sing.

The campaign is called "Bringing the Outside In." The BringingTheOutsideIn.org website is a marvel. The world-class design of the Center and its visionary outreach are Tybee crown jewels.

Addy will make her trip from the South End to the North End around Christmas, her journey a gift from a generous community. Next July she will be released to the sea with a birthday wish. In a generation may her ties to these sands and to many helping hands bring her back for a moonlight reunion.

43

Up a Tree

Tybee loves its trees. The city arborist knows them down to the bark. And he loves to roam through Jaycee Park.

43

Up a Tree

If you spend a little time with Tybee City arborist Brent Levy, you soon realize that he is seeing things. I don't mean he's hallucinating. I mean that he's seeing tree detail that we civilians can casually miss. He doesn't see the tree as a snapshot; he sees the movie.

While I see a tree in a general way, he sees the leaves, the bark, the roots, the bugs and birds it shelters. With X-ray vision he sees its roots, the nutrients and mycelial network in its soil, the water table on which it stands.

He took me on a short walk recently through one of his favorite places on earth - Tybee's Jaycee Park. Over the hour he touched probably a tree a minute.

He checked out the pruning of the pond cypress trees; he felt the texture of the reddish-brown needles that form a soft cushion beneath them. Pointing out the scores of century plant pups springing up along the parking lot, he was excited to see seedlings of cherry laurel.

He crushed some leaves to release the smell that gives them the name "Dr. Pepper trees." Then he cautioned me not to eat the berries. As we walked, he alternated between common and scientific names: Quercus virginiana, Magnolia grandiflora, Prunus caroliniana. I was relieved that he didn't begin calling me Homo sapiens.

Brent talked about a plan for educational tree signage throughout the park. "Good information elevates the experience. It gets you closer to nature. An educational component can go naturally with the aesthetic component."

The park is already family and recreation friendly. We walked along the pleasant winding half-mile trail. It is crisscrossed by the very popular 18-hole disc golf course, with challenging holes over water hazards and around palm trees.

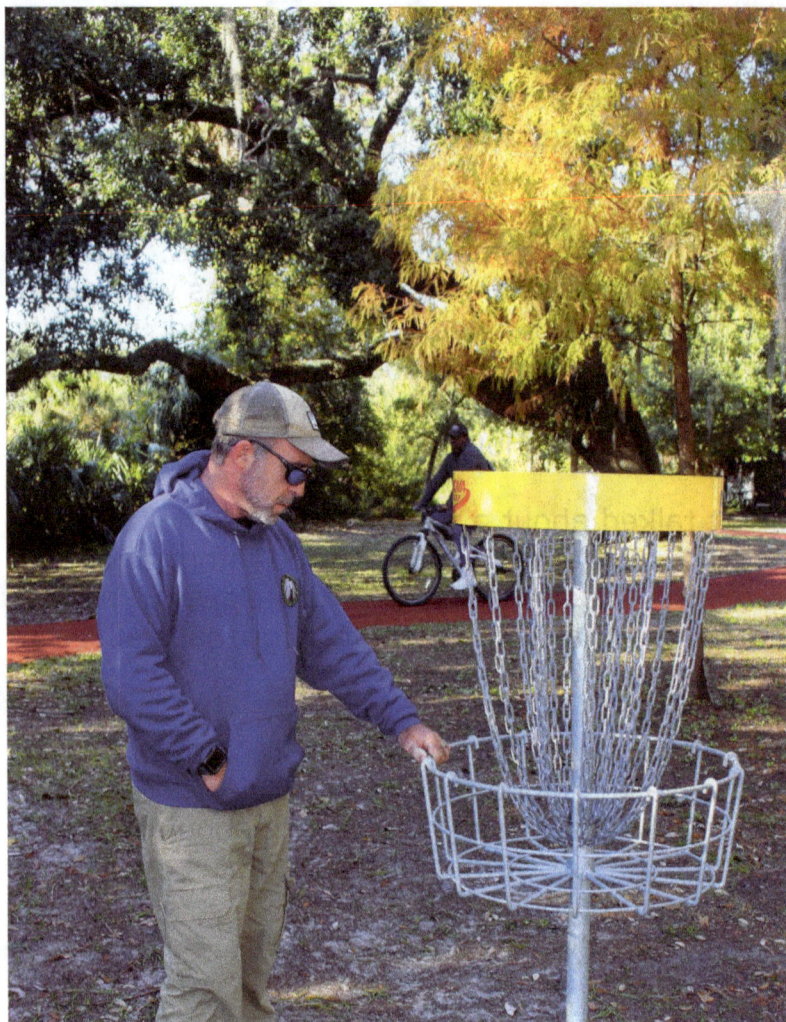

We watched a very patient white egret hunt for minnows among the cattails in the park's brackish ponds. The ponds are restful spots where kids and grown-ups catch small redfish. Some still mornings all you can hear are the splashes of juvenile tarpon rolling to gulp air.

Most days there are games being played on the pickle ball and basketball courts. Brent was especially proud of the fenced children's playground

with cooling shade covers and a padded water-permeable surface. He mentioned too that the city will soon improve the turf of the soccer and baseball fields.

"This park is an 11-acre gem. It's an oasis. Lots of artists set up to paint here, and the park gazebo is a popular wedding spot."

Brent is really partial to the park's live oaks. He had just come from doing a health assessment of an ancient oak in Isle of Hope. "It is showing signs of die-back. It's producing more shoots and acorns, not to extend its own life, but to insure future generations of its species."

At walk's end, I ran into Arnie Seyden, another big fan of the park. He was head of the Jaycees when the park was built in the 1960's.

The park's history is family history to him. Beneath centerfield lies a 15-feet tall concrete foundation for the fort's garrison flagpole. 50,000 cubic yards of fill built up the swampy areas. 49 palm trees were relocated to Savannah's southside. In 1932 Post commander George Marshall's wife Katherine planted the crepe myrtle trees along the park's eastern border.

Brent is proud of Tybee's association with the Savannah Tree Foundation and Arbor Day, and those bonds are about to get stronger. He recently joined the board of the Georgia Tree Council. "I can't wait to network with people across the state who care about trees as much as I do."

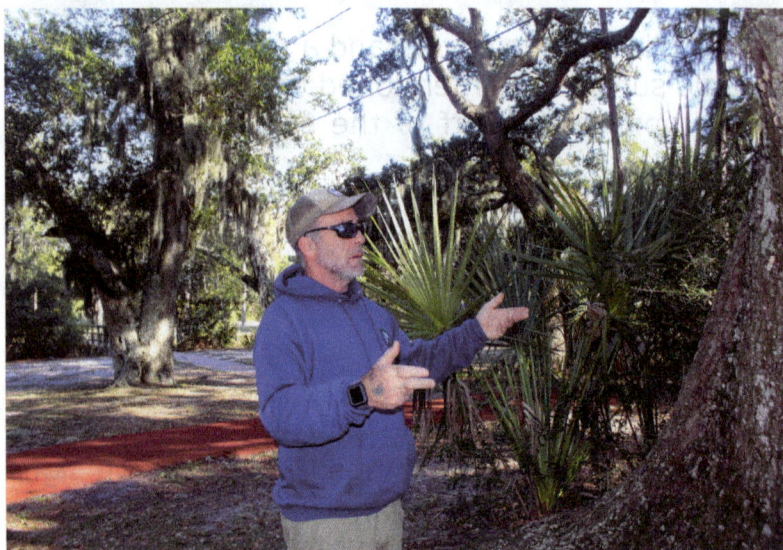

INDEX

i

Name	Chapter

Name	Chapter

Name	Chapter

Name	Chapter

Name	Chapter

Name	Chapter

Name	Chapter

Name	Chapter

APPENDIX

www.ingramcontent.com/pod-product-compliance
Lightning Source LLC
Chambersburg PA
CBHW062117020426
42335CB00013B/999